"Some books you read, and others, well, they read you. Marilyn's book does just that. And some books inspire, others educate, but few motivate you to put those feelings to action. Marilyn's book does this too. Her analogies and word pictures don't just spark a different way of thinking, they spark a different way of becoming. Her words stay with you and demand something to change as a response. *Beyond the Enneagram* came into my life before I even knew I fully needed it, just like spiritually attuned best friends seem to do."

—Krista Breilh, founder of Live Salted, a movement equipping authentic, bold, and compelling disciple makers

"Marilyn has taken us to a deeper place with *Beyond the Enneagram* whereby we can begin to understand that our journey is not only to discover who we are but also to move toward healing of what's been lost along the way. Four years ago, sitting across a café table from her, I remember the moment she said, "I want people to be healed at a deep level. God wants to lead us toward wholeness." Her conviction runs true in this new book of her own evolving faith, given to us in a simple and profound manner through the use of her unique diagram and personal stories."

—Mary Pandiani, D.Min., executive director of Selah Center

"In sensing something significant missing from the model of the Enneagram as we've known it, Marilyn has expanded it to reflect its intent, as she says, 'to experience a more centered and free life with God and to live more fully as the person you were created to be.' *Beyond the Enneagram* is a fresh approach that challenges the reader to face and journey along both the inward transformation and outward expression of who God created us to be and to enjoy a more centered life with God."

—Beth McCord, Founder and CCO, Your Enneagram Coach

"Marilyn Vancil has done it again. Her book, *Beyond the Enneagram*, is a must-read for all of us who want to do more than understand our Enneagram numbers. Marilyn has the 'posture of a pilgrim,' and from the confident cadence of her steady walk with God, she offers us this beautiful invitation: God is actively drawing us into a centered life where we fully and freely experience the perfect, transforming, love relationship of the Trinity. Thanks to Marilyn's practical, relatable wisdom from her own journey with God, we're invited to 'come further in.' And after realizing the true vision of God's heart for us from the beginning, one question remains: What are we waiting for?"

—Adam Ormond, executive director of Grafted Life Ministries

"Marilyn Vancil has done it again. Her first book, *Self to Lose, Self to Find,* has proven to be an invaluable resource for our Identity Exchange Seminars, but now her second work, *Beyond the Enneagram,* takes us to an even deeper spiritual level. It will now be required reading for all our courses."

—Jamie Winship, co-founder of Identity Exchange and author of *Living Fearless*

"Marilyn's *Self to Lose, Self to Find* was the very first book I ever read on the Enneagram. As a Christian, I loved the simple-yet-profound approach to the Enneagram through a Christian perspective. *Beyond the Enneagram* is an even more innovative work, centered around a new diagram called The Drawing which visually lays out our protective strategies, false beliefs, and more that get in the way of experiencing our union with God. If you are a Christian who loves the Enneagram and wants to pursue deeper transformation, this is the next step! Reading this book felt like sitting down and having a conversation with a wise sage who was delighted to share a lifetime of valuable lessons and timeless truths."

—Tyler Zach, pastor and author of *The Gospel For Enneagram* devotional series

"This book is a holy, helpful work of art! With tender care, Marilyn invites those of us who may have felt boxed in by the Enneagram to remember (and maybe see for the first time) how limitations tend to lead to abundance in our stories. If you are someone like me who is tempted to discard trends, I beg you to reconsider by taking a deeper look 'beyond the Enneagram' (with Marilyn as your guide), toward a more whole and centered perspective with this ancient tool that, when used well, leads us Home to the One who made us all in His image."

—Meredith McDaniel, MA, LCMHC, author of *In Want + Plenty*

"This new work by Marilyn Vancil is a powerful, breathtaking gold mine for every Christian seeking all that God has in store. Filled with paradigm-shifting insights and quotes, framed creatively and thoughtfully to walk the reader through step by reflective step—I look forward to recommending this book to every leader I know!"

—Rev. Sue Nilson Kibbey, director, Bishop Bruce Ough Innovation Center, United Theological Seminary, Dayton, Ohio

BEYOND THE
ENNEAGRAM

BEYOND
THE
ENNEAGRAM

AN INVITATION TO EXPERIENCE
A MORE CENTERED LIFE WITH GOD

Marilyn Vancil

CONVERGENT

NEW YORK

Published in the United States by Convergent Books,
an imprint of Random House, a division of
Penguin Random House LLC, New York.

CONVERGENT BOOKS is a registered trademark and its C colophon
is a trademark of Penguin Random House LLC.

All Scripture quotations, unless otherwise indicated, are taken
from the Holy Bible, New International Version®, NIV®.
Copyright © 1973, 1978, 1984, 2011 by Biblica, Inc.™ Used by
permission of Zondervan. All rights reserved worldwide.
www.zondervan.com The "NIV" and "New International
Version" are trademarks registered in the United States
Patent and Trademark Office by Biblica, Inc.™.

Enneagram drawing by Brooke Levine

LIBRARY OF CONGRESS CATALOGING-IN-PUBLICATION DATA
Names: Vancil, Marilyn, author.
Title: Beyond the Enneagram / Marilyn Vancil.
Description: New York : Convergent, [2022] | Includes
bibliographical references.
Identifiers: LCCN 2022021431 (print) | LCCN 2022021432 (ebook) |
ISBN 9780593236857 (hardback) | ISBN 9780593236864 (ebook)
Subjects: LCSH: Enneagram—Religious aspects—Christianity. |
Personality—Religious aspects—Christianity.
Classification: LCC BV4597.57 .V355 2022 (print) |
LCC BV4597.57 (ebook) | DDC 248.4—dc23/eng/20220610
LC record available at https://lccn.loc.gov/2022021431
LC ebook record available at https://lccn.loc.gov/2022021432

PRINTED IN THE UNITED STATES OF AMERICA ON ACID-FREE PAPER

crownpublishing.com

2 4 6 8 9 7 5 3 1

FIRST EDITION

Book design by Dana Leigh Blanchette

Dedicated to my dear husband, Jeff,
in the fiftieth year of our marriage.
My one and only love.

I am blessed beyond words
to live life with you!

Come, all you who are thirsty,
   come to the waters . . .
Listen, listen to me, and eat what is good,
   and you will delight in the richest of fare.
Give ear and come to me;
   listen, that you may live.

   —ISAIAH 55:1–3

CONTENTS

INTRODUCTION

I have come home at last! This is my real country! I belong here. This is the land I have been looking for all my life, though I never knew it till now. . . . Come further up, come further in!

—C. S. LEWIS, *THE LAST BATTLE*

Our greatest need then is to return to the deep center of our being where God's very self is present to us in cruciform love as our true being.

—M. ROBERT MULHOLLAND JR., *THE DEEPER JOURNEY*

One of my favorite pieces of jewelry is a silver spiral-shaped pendant my dear friend Julie gave me upon her return from a trip to Ireland. I wear it often as a necklace, particularly when I'm meeting with someone for spiritual direction or speaking at workshops and retreats. I love this pendant, not only because it reminds me of my special friendship with Julie, but also because of what the shape symbolizes. In the Celtic tradition, this "single spiral" represents growth, expansion, and the flow of life both inwardly and outwardly. I view it as a beautiful and fitting depiction of the spiritual journey toward a more centered life with God: the movement from the outer ego to the interior space of the soul where intimacy with God is enjoyed, and the movement outward to express God's love in the world and to serve others. This captures what I long to experience more deeply and consistently for myself and for those I meet with and guide.

Circles and spirals have frequently been used to symbolize the spiritual life and the interior movements of the soul toward the divine. Saint Teresa of Ávila, while seeking to understand the dynamics of prayer and a relationship with God, received a vision of a "magnificent castle inside our own souls, at the center of which the Beloved himself dwells. . . . From the center of the soul . . . God is calling. The driving force of our existence is our longing to find our way home to him."[1]

Father Thomas Keating, one of the founders of Contemplative Outreach, frequently used the image of a spiraling staircase in his video series on *The Psychological Experience of Centering Prayer,* signifying what he called "divine therapy," in which a person's pilgrimage toward a freer and fuller experience of life narrows and cycles toward the immovable One at the center.

Another well-known ancient circular structure is the labyrinth, which has long been used as a meditation and prayer tool, representing a journey to one's own center with God and a return to the outside world.

I came upon a labyrinth that took my breath away while hiking in the woods above a retreat center. The wall of the spiraling circle was built with sheared tree limbs, and in the center was a large copper kettle filled with water, reflecting the sky and trees above. My walk toward the center felt truly holy as I slowed my pace, breathed deeply, and took in the beauty and quiet around me. When I stopped in the middle and looked into the water, I saw my own face reflected back and sensed the sacredness of my own personhood as a reflection of God's image and a participant in God's larger world. As is usually the case when I take a slow meditative walk along a labyrinth, I felt settled as I journeyed outward, and I left with a renewed awareness of God's love, presence, and guidance.

And then, we have the Enneagram.

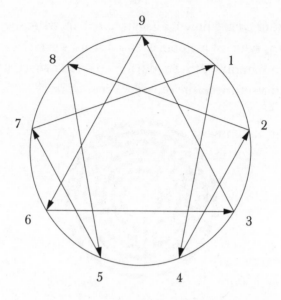

The circular symbol, as we know it today, with connecting lines and nine numbers around the perimeter, was introduced to the modern world in the early 1900s by George Gurdjieff, a philosopher and spiritual teacher who had encountered the Enneagram at some point in his search for ancient wisdom about human transformation. Where he learned it is unclear, but it became a main focus of his work. According to Enneagram teachers Don Richard Riso and Russ Hudson, "The system that Gurdjieff taught was a vast and complex study of psychology, spirituality, and cosmology that aimed at helping students understand their objective purpose in life. Gurdjieff also taught that the Enneagram was the central and most important symbol in his philosophy."[2] Many of the components included in Enneagram teachings today, particularly the psychological elements, were *not* part of Gurdjieff's work, but were added by others later.

I've studied the Enneagram for more than three decades, and it has been an invaluable tool for my personal growth. In my first book, *Self to Lose, Self to Find: Using the Enneagram to Uncover Your True, God-Gifted Self,* I shared my own journey with the Enneagram, along with an explanation of the Enneagram system within a biblical context, descriptions of the nine Enneagram types, prayers for each one, and a practical pathway for applying the knowledge of one's type to live more fully and freely.

However, this second book, *Beyond the Enneagram,* is *not* about the Enneagram, but rather about the *intent* of the Enneagram as I view it: to experience a more centered and free life with God and to live more fully as the person you were created to be.

Why not another Enneagram book? Because I've sensed for a while now that something significant is missing from the original Enneagram drawing, a missing perspective that goes beyond what this map of the human experience offers. We need a more complex picture of inner transformation and soul restoration. For a model that is widely considered a spiritual tool, it's notable that there are no clear representations of the spirit on the current Enneagram symbol. The intelligences of the head, heart, and body are included, but where is the intelligence of the spirit recognized? Although many valuable and insightful elements have been developed to fit on the symbol Gurdjieff used, the image itself hasn't changed. It's still a circle with nine points and lines connecting those points. As a result, attempting to explain and encounter the breadth and depth of spiritual transformation using the existing construct has limitations.

I believe an expanded and enhanced model is needed. What I propose here is a new image and an added perspective, an adjunct to the Enneagram that includes its wisdom, but also focuses inwardly toward the center space and extends beyond the existing circle to include more about the human experience. To borrow a phrase from C. S. Lewis, we're all invited to *come further in* to a more centered and intimate life with God. We are also called to live out the actualization of what this means in our everyday lives. This fresh approach includes both the inward movement and the outward expression, facilitating a greater comprehension of our sacred spiritual pilgrimage toward reclaiming our truest, God-gifted self and experiencing a more centered life with God.

This new image has a simple name: *The Drawing*. Below is a simplified version that I'll explain thoroughly in chapter 6. I named it *The Drawing* for two reasons. It's an actual drawing, but, more significantly, it depicts the holy attraction (the drawing) of our spirits toward God's Spirit as the ultimate destiny and desire of our lives. As Evelyn Underhill describes it, "We are drawn almost in spite of ourselves—not as a result of our own over-anxious struggles—to the real end of our being, the place where we are ordained to be: a journey which is more like the inevitable movement of the iron filings to the great magnet that attracts it, than like the long and weary pilgrimage."[3]

As with the other examples of spirals and circles to illustrate the spiritual life, the primary movement of *The Drawing* is toward the middle space, our Spiritual Center, the transcendent way of knowing beyond the more commonly recognized Centers of the Gut, Heart, and Head used to categorize the Enneagram types. In *Self to Lose, Self to Find,* I wrote about the reality of this Spiritual Center and my placement of it in the middle of the Enneagram image. The following paragraphs from that book set the stage for the explanation of *The Drawing*:

> *I direct your attention to the open space in the middle of the Enneagram, suggesting this represents our spiritual union with God, the true Center of who we are. We have a Spiritual Intelligence, or what could be called our Inner Knowing. As indicated in 1 Corinthians 2:11, the knowing of our thoughts is linked to our spirits: "For who knows a person's thoughts except their own spirit within them? In the same way no one knows the thoughts of God except the Spirit of God."*
>
> *What exactly is our spirit? . . . Many theologians define the "soul" as the combination of our emotions, mind, and will—our heart, head, and gut. They then define the "spirit" as the innermost part where God dwells, where we are in union with the Divine and where we spiritually discern the deeper truths of life. Thus, our spiritual intelligence and our union with God are vital aspects of who we are and are critical to the process of our spiritual formation.*
>
> *How does this relate to the Enneagram? Look at the Enneagram drawing. Now imagine a tight fist at each of the nine points around the circle. These fists symbolize the grip of the compulsive and distorted*

nature of each type pattern, similar to the seed coat that doesn't want to be released. When our Adapted Self clings to all our self-protective and unredeemed ways of being, we can be closed, stuck, and unreceptive to God's love and direction.

Now imagine a burst of light in the middle of the drawing. This center space represents the loving union of our spirit with God's Spirit and the place where the fullness of God dwells within us. When we loosen our grip and let go as God draws us toward this center, we gain spiritual "knowing," which is connected and aligned with the love and presence of God's heart, mind, and will.[4]

For a clear comprehension of *The Drawing* and its value for the spiritual life, some important foundations need to be in place. I lay these foundations in section I. Chapter 1 reviews the need and process for "Inner Soul Restoration," a key for unlocking our capacity to experience fully and freely our lives as God intended them to be. Chapter 2 explains "The Posture of a Pilgrim," the essential nature of our lifelong journey toward wholeness, freedom, and a more centered life with God. Chapter 3 highlights "Signposts Along the Way," the stages of faith we pass through on our spiritual pilgrimage. Lastly, I describe similar "Stages on the Enneagram Journey" in chapter 4, examining when the use of the Enneagram can be valuable and when it may cease to be useful or needed along the spiritual path.

Section II unveils the meaning and details of *The Drawing*, starting in chapter 5 with a comparison of "Bounded

Set and Centered Set Perspectives." Chapter 6, "*The Draw-ing* Explained," describes the components of *The Drawing* and their significance for understanding and responding to the sacred invitation to *come further in*.

Section III gets personal, practical, and especially perti-nent for our spiritual growth as we're drawn toward the center of our union with God. In *Self to Lose, Self to Find,* I explained that we have two selves, one I termed the Adapted Self and the other, the Authentic Self. The former, the Adapted Self, was formed in our early years. We adopted self-protective and self-development strategies that helped us get along in the world, ones we perceived would ensure that our basic human needs for love and affection, safety and security, and power and control were met. The other, our Authentic Self, is our original and truest self, created to experience and express divine attributes of God's image in a unique way. This Authentic Self is usually hidden under the layers of the Adapted Self, a reality I illustrated as a seed coat protecting and covering a true seed inside. When we gradually release the outer seed coat of our Adapted Self patterns, we then create more space for our inner Au-thentic Self to be reclaimed and to become more flourishing and fruitful.

This shift from the strategies of our Adapted Self to the manifestations of our Authentic Self is the journey of spir-itual transformation. We move *from* various states of an ego-focused existence *to* sacred ways of being—*from* self-orientation *to* God-centered living. I elaborate on seven of these sacred shifts in Section III, each expressed in the con-text of scriptural truths and real-life experiences. The first six movements, listed below, are explored in Chapters 7 through 12:

From What I Am *to* Who I Am
From Reactive *to* Responsive
From Bondage *to* Freedom
From Wounded *to* Whole
From Shakable *to* Unshakable
From Burdened *to* Rested

The final chapter is my favorite—"*From* Glory *to* Glory"! It encompasses all of these movements and is the most hopeful and consequential truth you could ever realize about your divine destiny as one who is invited by God to *come further in.*

In conclusion, I offer some Closing Thoughts, bringing all of the book's content full circle and back to the original intent of this book: to encourage you, my readers, to receive and respond to the holy invitation to experience and enjoy a more centered life with God.

As I set out to write this book, I had a general sense of the message I felt called to communicate, but had no idea how it would develop and take shape. I knew I wanted to explore the nature of inner soul restoration and spiritual transformation. I also knew I wanted to offer a fresh perspective and a new paradigm that would include the Enneagram, but expand beyond it. Following a few fits and starts, I realized I lacked a clear understanding of the book's purpose and process; I needed an image that would help me organize my thoughts and direction. The picture that came

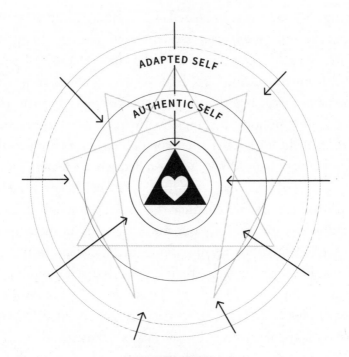

THE DRAWING

to me was a "pot of soup," a collection of ingredients that would blend and simmer to create a nourishing and satiating "meal" for those who were hungry for more in their spiritual lives.

I shared this image in an email to the "gal pals" who lovingly pray for me as I write. The first person to respond was Julie Jensen, my dear friend who gave me the spiral pendant. She shared that "the best soups I make are when I use ingredients I already have on hand, adding a few spices and herbs to bring out the flavors." Julie had no idea how much this message would impact how I approached this book and how it has evolved into this final outcome. After pondering her message, I realized that all I could offer in *Beyond the Enneagram* was what I already had in the "pantry" of my own life, the ingredients that have shaped me into who I am today. So, I pulled favorite resources from my bookshelf, gathered favorite excerpts from my favorite authors, and pondered some of my favorite scriptures. I thumbed through journals, remembered the many people who have influenced me, and recalled what I name "Holy Aha" experiences that were turning points in my life. To add extra flavors and enhance the content, I reviewed conversations with others about breakthroughs in their lives, and asked them for permission to include their stories in my simmering soup (with their names changed of course).

What you now have is my "pot of soup," the combination of ingredients I gathered, prepared, chopped up, mixed together, and let simmer for the last few years.

I'm forever grateful to Julie for writing her insightful message, and even more so now—it was one of the last texts she sent me before she was too weakened by cancer and sadly passed away. So, thank you, Julie, dear friend: your life, your love, and your legacy are woven throughout the pages of this book.

And, I pray, as Julie would have prayed, that all who partake of this "meal" will be warmed, nourished, strengthened, and sustained for their ongoing pilgrimages toward enjoying more centered lives with God.

Bon appétit!

SECTION I

Foundations for the Journey

May you travel in an awakened way,
Gathered wisely into your inner ground;
That you may not waste the invitations
Which wait along the way to transform you.

—JOHN O'DONOHUE, "FOR THE TRAVELER"

CHAPTER 1

Inner Soul Restoration

And the God of all grace, who called you to his eternal glory in Christ, after you have suffered a little while, will himself restore you and make you strong, firm and steadfast.

—1 PETER 5:10

To ask to be healed is an incredibly courageous thing, because we will then be taken into a world that we know not and we will be stretched and challenged to make our living in a new way, not off our pathologies, but from our health.

—PARKER J. PALMER, AS QUOTED BY CATHERINE WHITMIRE
IN *PRACTICING PEACE*

Visualize with me a beautiful handcrafted chair, constructed from the finest wood and assembled with masterful and flawless workmanship. Admire the intricate carvings that adorn the elegant back. Imagine sitting in the comfortable seat shaped into just the right contours. Notice the deep and rich luster of the wood brought out by the soft and smooth finish. Marvel at the splendor of this irreplaceable and priceless work of art, lovingly and carefully created by a master artisan.

Now imagine this chair, years after it was made, in the corner of a dusty and cramped garage, buried under disorderly stuff and seemingly useless to anyone who might find it. The wood is covered over with layers of paint, an arm is dangling loose, another seems to be missing, the leg joints are loose and wobbly, the carvings are indistinguishable, and the wood is etched with deep and damaging grooves.

In order to recapture its initial and authentic beauty, the chair must undergo a rigorous yet gentle process of restoration. A skillful and dedicated woodworker, who imagines and appreciates the original masterpiece and sees beyond the damage and layers of paint, would need to take on the extensive endeavor of reclaiming its former glory. If you've ever stripped layers of paint from furniture, you know what this involves: solvent, scraping, sanding, more solvent, more scraping, and more sanding over and over until the paint is removed, the wood is smooth, and the grain shines through again.

Replacing lost parts and reconnecting all the pieces presents a very real challenge. Although the new parts will never exactly replicate the original ones, a careful and adept carpenter can create a close match. Flaws will remain, but they will give the newly restored chair a distinctive look with its own form of beauty and an expression of its unique history. The final coat of penetrating oil or lacquer will preserve and protect the wood and give it a lustrous sheen. At

long last, the furniture restorer will stand back and celebrate with satisfaction that the chair once again fulfills its
original design as an exquisite one-of-a-kind work of art,
beautiful to behold and a comfortable place to rest.

With this image in mind, let's look at what the complex
process of "inner soul restoration" involves and why we
need it to more fully experience a centered life with God.
Like the metaphorical chair, we've each been changed from
our original sacred design by the life experiences we've
encountered and endured. Being restored to our original
undamaged condition may seem appealing and desirable—
something we long for—but it's also daunting to think of
being sanded, scraped, and repaired. What does it really
mean, and what might the work of restoration entail? Although the mystery of soul transformation will always be
more than our finite minds and limited experiences can
grasp, we can gain some initial insights by taking a look at
these three words: *Inner. Soul. Restoration.*

Inner. The process of true soul renewal takes place in our
inner life. It's not about redecorating the old self or gluing
the "seed coat" of the Adapted Self back in place. Managing
behaviors and exercising self-discipline are important and
may alter some habits and change our ways, but that's not
enough. If our inner life—where memories, wounds, false
narratives, and habitual self-protective patterns reside—is
not addressed, then long-lasting change is unlikely.

W. Ian Thomas, in his book *If I Perish, I Perish,* uses a
humorous and striking analogy—attempting to domesti-
cate a pig—in order to explain the futility of trying to
change ourselves by altering our outer life without an in-

ward transformation. Thomas uses a phrase that still reverberates in my mind from this hypothetical story: "Pig is pig." The author invites us to imagine he decides to adopt a pig to prove his belief that pigs have been misjudged and that they wallow in the mud only because of their unsatisfactory environment and insufficient upbringing. He feels that with proper training and attire, a pig can change and develop better character and live a more acceptable life. The pig is dressed in little blue pants, is taught to wipe its feet, learns to sit at the table, and how to sleep between clean sheets. All is going well, and it seems the little pig is converting to a more desirable life, until someone leaves the door open and the pig gets a whiff of the outdoors. It hurries outside. "Reaching the muddiest bog it can find, the little pig plunges in, and after rolling over and over, it lies on its back in the mud, little blue pants and all. With a delightful grin on its face, and with its feet sticking up in the air, it cries at the top of its voice, 'Home, sweet home.'"[1]

Thomas explains the point of this allegory: "It is absolutely imperative for your own spiritual well-being that you recognize the fact that this old nature will never change its character. All the wickedness of which it is capable today, it will be capable of tomorrow—or for that matter fifty years from now."[2] Our natural proclivity is to go back to the mudhole when we have the chance. This may sound a bit harsh, but this truth is actually quite a relief. We don't need to dress up our old self, train it to behave, embark on rigorous self-improvement plans, bury our hurts, deny our shortcomings, and live as if our Adapted Self persona is all we've got. True transformation happens not on the outside but in our inner being where the Spirit of Christ dwells, guides, and restores us. Thomas ends his "Pig Is Pig" chapter with these instructive words: "It is only when you are honest enough to face up to these facts, that you will have, on the one hand, a big enough view of what the Lord Jesus came into the world to do for you; and on the other hand, the desire to let Him do it!"[3]

Soul. In my quest to find a good definition of *soul*, I encountered many different attempts to narrow this mysterious part of us to a simple and clear understanding. One's soul is generally defined as a composite of one's mind, will, and emotions. Tilden Edwards, in his book on spiritual direction, was especially helpful because he combines the reality of the human soul with the impossibility of fully comprehending what it is. He opens with this reflection: "Perhaps the greatest paradox of human life is the discovery that what is most substantial about us is most elusive. I am speaking of our deep souls, that essence of our being that transcends but is integrally part of all our visible dimensions of body, will, mind, and feelings."[4] Further, he says, "For all its fuzziness, the word *soul* strikes a deep resonance in many people, as though our hearts know what it means, even if our minds can't fully grasp it."[5] The topic of the soul gets even trickier when we endeavor to distinguish it from the spirit; I'm not even going to try to do that!

For the purposes of this book, I won't attempt to explain the soul, but instead offer, as it relates to the subject at hand, this conclusion: *Our souls need restoration.* Our minds need renewal, our wills need bridling, and our hearts need mending.

Why is this so? Because our souls are damaged, distorted, and disregarded like the handcrafted chair we imagined earlier. Even though our Master Creator fashioned us to live freely and fully as stunning masterpieces, we are in "the corner of the garage" in a variety of ways and in varying degrees. Some of us have suffered great trauma and loss, while others have endured subtle hurts. I don't need to cite statistics to prove this is true. We know it within us, and we see it all around us. The outward manifestations of our inner soul stories show up in numerous ways, from withdrawal to aggression, from overachieving to underachieving, from resignation to rebellion, from one form of reactivity to another.

None of us are completely destroyed like the chair I described earlier, or we wouldn't be here. We've managed to survive and thrive in many courageous ways, and we've experienced love, beauty, joy, hope, and gifts of grace. Each of us can look with gratitude at the goodness of life and the many blessings we've known. And we should—gratitude is so vital to our well-being.

Yet, our one-of-a kind "soul art" is buried beneath piles of experiences and perceptions of life events, whether we're aware of it or not. We often don't even know why we do what we do, feel what we feel, and think what we think. We operate on autopilot without any cognizance of what lurks beneath the surface of our consciousness, influencing our state of being more than we even realize. Pressures to perform and make our way in the world have weighed down our truest and best selves. Layers of memories, both recalled and suppressed, pleasant and unpleasant, have covered over the simple beauty of our authentic souls. Injustice and mistreatment have gouged once-innocent lives. Some carry deep grief over painful wounds and losses. Choices have left us with regrets. Self-protective strategies and defensiveness have diminished openness to God and others. Anxiety, insecurity, and fears have developed from broken hearts, unfulfilled dreams, and silent hurts. Bitterness, lack of forgiveness, judgment, and anger have etched harmful grooves in relationships. False assumptions and distorted inner narratives have skewed our true identities, and we have looked for validation in all the wrong places. Our souls have been impacted by our lived experiences in varying degrees of intensity and in a multitude of ways. This is the common human condition.

Beneath the many layers of our story is an even deeper story. All of us, consciously or unconsciously, long to be connected to the Source of life, where we can know true fulfillment, unconditional love, and peace. Whether we acknowledge it or not, our souls cry out for healing and wholeness with both subtle and loud expressions. The Psalmist echoes our deepest yearnings:

O God, you are my God;
I earnestly search for you.
My soul thirsts for you;
my whole body longs for you
in this parched and weary land
where there is no water.
—*Psalm 63:1 (NLT)*

Restoration. The Merriam-Webster online definition for *restoration* is "the act or an instance of bringing something damaged or worn back to its original state."[6] Given this understanding, soul restoration is the process of bringing us back, as close as possible, to our original state of being whole, unwounded, expansive, and a priceless one-of-a-kind masterpiece. How then can this happen? How can we reclaim and return to our truest Authentic Self, living freely and fully both inwardly and outwardly? How can our damaged and worn condition be repaired and revitalized?

Just as with the chair illustration, restoration requires work. And it takes time. There is no way around this. Our heavy burdens must be lifted. The solvent of truth must dissolve layers of deceptions and perceptions. Painful memories need to be revisited and healed so they can be scraped away. False identities must be sanded off so that the "true grain" of the Authentic Self can shine through once again. The small nicks and deep gouges of hurts and wounds need to be patched up with healing balms of compassion and grace. And the penetrative oil of love must be applied to preserve and protect the newly restored and tender soul. It's an ongoing process, a pilgrimage, one that takes a lifetime to complete and one that will not be fully realized until we enjoy our final home in heaven.

Unlike an inanimate chair, we humans are complex and mysterious. Reclaiming our truest self is much more than a one-time spiritual revelation or breakthrough. Prayer, reading the scriptures, and engaging in worship are invaluable and necessary practices for our spiritual vibrancy, but change doesn't happen overnight. Using the Enneagram and other personality assessments as tools to scrape off layers of our false selves is useful, but these systems can't heal us. Intentional practices and concentrated efforts to reform ourselves can surely help, but they won't unravel the mystery, depth, and complexity of our inner stories. Spiritual direction, therapy, mentoring, pastoral care, and instruction serve as essential guides, but they alone can't provide true and lasting restoration.

Returning to our chair example, the key figure in the transformative work of repair and restoration is the skillful, loving, and dedicated artisan who desires, above all else, to reclaim the original beauty and unique splendor of the broken object. This is a picture of our loving Creator, the One who knows us best, the One who sees our broken and wounded places and knows just what we need to be restored, and the One who longs to draw us back to the original condition of our true and Authentic Self. The Scriptures are filled with pictures and promises of God's desires for us, and of what we can know and experience under the gentle love and restorative work of our gracious God.

One such picture of restoration is portrayed in Isaiah 35. At a time of personal difficulty in my own life, when I was questioning my value and experiencing a sense of rejection and uncertainty, I read and reread this passage, clinging desperately to the promise of wholeness and joy, even though I was hurting and lost. The entire passage became my source of peace and hope that God would restore me eventually. The following few lines were particularly poignant for me:

The desert and the parched land will be glad;
    the wilderness will rejoice and blossom.
Like the crocus, it will burst into bloom;
    it will rejoice greatly and shout for joy. (35:1–2)

Those the Lord has rescued will return.
They will enter Zion with singing;
    everlasting joy will crown their heads.
Gladness and joy will overtake them,
    and sorrow and sighing will flee away. (35:10)

God desires to restore our souls, and is the One who promises to do it for us. Even though we have traveled through parched places and endured rough seasons of difficult circumstances, God desires to bring us back to our original Authentic Selves, to a state of flourishing and fullness. God provides a way for gladness and joy to overtake us, and for our sorrow and sighing to flee. God will guide us and heal us. As the Psalmist says, "Though you have made me see troubles, many and bitter, *you will restore my life again;* from the depths of the earth you will again bring me up. You will increase my honor and comfort me once more" (Psalm 71:20–21, italics mine).

You may wonder, then, what your part is in the process of being restored, of reclaiming your Authentic Self. Since each of us has a unique and individual story requiring a personal pilgrimage, there are no set steps or formulas to follow. However, some common elements—similar to solvents, scrub brushes, scrapers, sandpaper, and finishing oils—are pertinent to all journeys of soul restoration. These are: *Desire. Willingness. Courage. Honesty. Trust.*

Desire. A deep-down honest desire to change and experience a new way of living is a crucial first step. Many whom Jesus touched and healed were desperate for relief from their sufferings, not just from physical ailments but from emotional and relational brokenness as well. They knew they were sick, they were honest about their frailty, they were weary of their pain, and they were tired of their alienation. People reached out to Him, were brought to Him, and encountered Him, all with the ardent desire to be healed and to experience true wholeness and restored lives.

Bruce Larson, former senior pastor of a Seattle church in the 1980s, shared in a sermon about a dear friend who operated a center where people came to be restored. Above the fireplace at this center was a sign that read, DO YOU WANT TO BE RIGHT OR DO YOU WANT TO BE WELL? This intriguing question was the foundation of the center's work in helping people receive the healing they desperately desired and needed.[7] Jesus asked a similar question of the man at the pool of Bethesda, who had been waiting for thirty-eight years for someone to come and help him into the healing water. "When Jesus saw him lying there and learned that he had been in this condition for a long time, he asked him, 'Do you want to get well?'" (John 5:6). We need to ask ourselves this critical question: Do I *really want* to undergo restoration, or would I rather "stay by the pool," clinging to excuses, blaming other people, living as a victim, justifying myself, and coping on my own with my limitations and suffering? Do I truly *desire* to be well and free?

Willingness. Our metaphorical chair is an inanimate object and has no choice but to go through the process of restoration, and will endure it without any pain or resistance. We humans are not so passive or impervious to the rigors of being restored. Most often, being ready and willing to submit ourselves to the work and process of inner soul restoration is not easy or natural. It requires a lot from us.

The willingness to pause and notice is crucial. Several years ago, my husband, Jeff, and I embarked on a week-long raft trip down the Copper River in Alaska with two dear friends and two experienced guides. We had no idea how dangerous this would be, especially considering the frigid river was as high as it had been in twenty years; falling into it would likely mean death. I bring this up to illustrate the necessity of paying attention, of intentionally noticing. Our guides watched the flow of the river constantly, looking for places where the water swirled around and flowed back upstream against the current. These eddies indicated something was below the surface, like a boulder or other obstruction, something that could puncture the raft or take us off course. Most eddies were minor, but some created powerful vortexes, called "boat eaters," that could trap our rafts in circles or suck them under.

To be restored to our true selves, we must be willing to notice and confess the "swirls" that take us out of the flow of God's Spirit within us. Life is full of eddies that can become "soul eaters" if we aren't paying attention. Some may seem minor, like a surge of envy or a desire to boast, and some may be major, like fits of rage or debilitating anxiety. Regardless of the magnitude of both the inward and outward reactions, they indicate something below the surface that needs to be heeded and healed in order to continue on our way to greater wholeness and freedom. We have to be willing to pause in order to recognize and admit when we're caught in a reactive vortex, and then look to our inner guide, the Spirit of the Living God, to show us the way through.

Tilden Edwards challenges us with these questions: "Are we willing to let whatever doesn't belong to divine freedom, love, and truth in us be purged as the Spirit sees we are ready, even if it leaves us disoriented and changed in ways we cannot predict? Do we want our deep soul to be nourished even if it empties us of everything with which we have identified as ultimately, rather than just relatively, who we are and what we need?"[8] In other words, we need to ask ourselves, "Am I *willing* to be changed no matter what it takes, where it will take me, and what I will need to yield to God?"

Courage. Since the path of restoration will not always be easy or quick, it requires courage and commitment. Repeating Parker Palmer's statement at the beginning of this chapter: "To ask to be healed is an incredibly courageous thing, because we will then be taken into a world that we know not and we will be stretched and challenged to make our living in a new way, not off our pathologies, but from our health."[9] That's a big statement!

The journey to soul restoration is not for the fainthearted or for those who want the easy and unexamined route toward freedom. It takes inner strength, perseverance, and bravery to invite healing and to face what might emerge and how we might be changed as we lay our souls wide open for God's healing touch. As C. S. Lewis wrote in *The Screwtape Letters*, "Courage is not simply one of the virtues but the form of every virtue at the testing point."[10]

The good news is that God's holy presence, love, and divine purposes will guide us along the path. And eventually the journey gets easier, and we'll experience more and more freedom and peace. "So do not fear, for I am with you; do not be dismayed, for I am your God. I will strengthen you and help you; I will uphold you with my righteous right hand" (Isaiah 41:10). Do you have the *courage* to allow God to restore you?

Honesty. Jesus told some of His new followers, "If you hold to my teaching, you are really my disciples. Then you will know the truth, and the truth will set you free" (John 8:31–32). What truth leads to freedom? Truth about Jesus. Truth about ourselves. Truth about our lives. The fisherman Peter expressed the combination of these truths when he looked with amazement at the miraculous load of fish in his boat because he followed the suggestion of Jesus to put his nets down in the water. "When Simon Peter saw this, he fell at Jesus' knees and said, 'Go away from me, Lord; I am a sinful man!'" (Luke 5:8). When he recognized the true identity of Jesus, Peter was honest about himself, his inadequacy, and the stark reality of his sinfulness. As we know, Peter became a friend and follower of Jesus, even though he stumbled at times, and he was a foundational figure in the proclamation of the gospel following the death and resurrection of Jesus. In his letter of encouragement to scattered believers who were suffering, Peter wrote, "And the God of all grace, who called you to his eternal glory in Christ, after you have suffered a little while, will himself restore you and make you strong, firm and steadfast" (1 Peter 5:10). He had firsthand experience of the restoring power of God, through Jesus, beginning when he fell in front of Jesus and honestly confessed the true condition of his inward soul.

We have to honestly face the truth about ourselves, and oftentimes this means uncovering personal habits and faults that make us uncomfortable and resistant. We don't like being wrong. We are quick to justify and defend ourselves. We'd rather blame others than take responsibility for our thoughts, feelings, and actions. We don't want to forgive. We'd rather be victims. Examining the limitations, fears, compulsions, strivings, attachments, and addictions that fester below the surface and spill over into our lives and relationships is not our natural inclination. And, even if we know we have a problem, confessing it to God and to those we have hurt is difficult. Additionally, exposing our hurtful history, facing our inner wounds, and bringing up memories that have been shut away can be frightening and disorienting. Telling the truth is hard. It's painful. It's unsettling. And, it's necessary for healing and restoration. As Richard Rohr says, "The Spirit of truth itself will always set you free, but first it will make you miserable."[11]

At a time in our marriage when I was consistently complaining and correcting, Jeff asked me why I was so angry. I replied, with a voice like Lucy from the *Peanuts* cartoon, "Who says I'm angry?" and I thought to myself, *Not me, I don't do angry!*

I tried to push Jeff's question out of my mind, but it kept resurfacing. I finally chose to consider the possibility that anger was simmering below the surface of my generally calm exterior. During a time of reflective prayer, I asked God to show me if and why I was angry. An image came into my mind of a tall tree being pulled out of the ground with the main root popping up through the dirt a long way in the distance. I also saw other smaller trees growing out of this root along the path. With this image came the recollection of specific patterns in our early years of marriage that I had not released and forgiven. The hurt I felt in that season had grown strong roots in my soul. With humility, I admitted to both God and Jeff that my anger over this hidden and harbored hurt had cropped up in many ways throughout our marriage, and that this bitter root was affecting the current "tree" of my life and relationships in ways I didn't even realize. I had to be honest about my anger, release the long-held hurt, and allow God to set me free from the toxic root. "Whoever conceals their sins does not prosper, but the one who confesses and renounces them finds mercy" (Proverbs 28:13). Are you ready to be *honest*?

Trust. So far, it may seem like this work of soul restoration demands too much and is nearly impossible. Why would we even want to place ourselves in a position to be scraped, sanded, taken apart, and reoriented to a new and different way of living? Will it even be worth it in the long run? It's understandable why we would resist submitting to this work when we don't have a sense of what we'll encounter, how much it will require, and how we'll end up.

Trust is *the* key reason we would even embark on this journey of soul healing. But where do we place our trust? Certainly not in ourselves, in other people, or in some kind of formula. Remember the expert and careful work of the craftsman who restored the damaged chair? The only One to trust is our loving and grace-filled Creator, whose purposes and desires for us are good and holy. We don't have to stress and strain to be restored; our work is to believe and surrender to God's guidance and life-giving love. We don't have to "dig up stuff"; God will show us where and what needs healing. We don't have to fear God's restoration project; God is not out to get us, but to reclaim our original design. "Trust in the Lord with all your heart and lean not on your own understanding. In all your ways, acknowledge Him and He will direct your paths" (Proverbs 3:5–6, NKJV).

One of my favorite verses in the Psalms is from Psalm 23: *"He leads me beside the still waters, he restores my soul."* This has always caught my attention because I know the delightful refreshment I experience whenever I stroll by quiet waters. However, I've not considered much why a sheep, the "voice" in Psalm 23, might need to be "restored," and how this might relate to my own soul restoration.

In his classic book, *A Shepherd Looks at Psalm 23,* W. Phillip Keller, a shepherd himself, gives us practical and relevant insights about the needs and habits of sheep in relation to the shepherd who cares for them. In the chapter on this verse about soul restoration, Keller explains the significance and potential harm of being a "cast down" sheep, which means that a sheep has turned over on its back and can't get back up without help. He describes it this way: "The 'cast' sheep is a very pathetic sight. Lying on its back, its feet in the air, it flays away frantically struggling to stand up, without success. Sometimes it will bleat for a little help, but generally it lies there lashing about in frightened frustration."[12] I don't know about you, but at times I can relate to the plight of this floundering animal.

Keller gives several reasons why a sheep would find itself in this vulnerable position. One reason a sheep becomes cast is if it carries too much wool and is burdened by such a heavy load. "Whenever I found that a sheep was being cast because it had too long and heavy a fleece, I soon took quick steps to remedy the situation. In short order I would shear it clean. . . . This was not always a pleasant process. Sheep do not enjoy being sheared, and it represents some hard work for the shepherd, but it must be done."[13]

Keller describes in great detail the sheep's ordeal and the tender care needed by the shepherd to get a cast sheep restored to an upright position. "Little by little the sheep would regain its equilibrium. By and by it would dash away to rejoin the others, set free from its fears and frustrations, given another chance to live a little longer."[14]

How does this relate to our personal inner soul restoration? Keller explains: "In dealing with our old self-life, there will come a day when the Master must take us in hand and apply a keen cutting edge of His Word to our lives. It may be an unpleasant business for a time. No doubt we'll struggle and kick about it. We may get a few cuts and wounds. *But what a relief when it is all over. Oh, the pleasure of being set free from ourselves! What a restoration!*[15] (emphasis mine).

In my work as a spiritual director, I'm privileged to witness holy moments of soul restoration for people who *desire* to be made whole, who are *willing* to pay attention to their inner eddies and respond to God's guidance, who are *courageous* enough to face their own underlying stories, who are *honest* about their brokenness and their sinfulness, and who *trust* in the One who will restore and redeem them. It's truly a holy honor to be in a "front-row seat" to hear about the love and work of God in the lives of these precious people.

One such person is Suzanne. She has experienced remarkable breakthroughs in her life over the time we've been meeting together. Her honest and dogged willingness to seek God, be honest, and go through whatever it might take to know more and more of God's "restoration plan" for her has been astounding to witness. One day she told me of an experience that "moved a huge boulder" in her soul, one that had created eddies throughout her life. She related that she had been born before her parents were married, which at the time was a secret shame for them and something they rarely talked about. For all of her life Suzanne carried the identity that she was "unwanted" and a "mistake." She didn't realize until she became an adult how much this had affected her sense of confidence, and that she had put up a shield of armor over her heart to toughen herself up. Through a series of events, a door opened for Suzanne to have a transparent conversation with her parents. It was very healing for all of them. While expressing her gratitude to God in prayer, Suzanne sensed God telling her, "You were *always* planned. I designed for you to be born precisely when you were. Suzanne, *only* good has come from this." As Suzanne told me this life-shifting story, she said, "I now sense a new identity and I feel lighter in everything. Layers and layers of shame are falling off, like one of those nesting dolls. I'm freer and more filled with joy, and I'm more able to connect with people in ways I haven't been able to do before." The masterpiece known as Suzanne was being reclaimed because of her *desire, willingness, courage, honesty,* and *trust in God.*

Similar Holy Aha moments of spiritual breakthroughs are also available for you if you seek them. And, once you taste the freedom, the lightness, the joy, the peace, and the emergence of your God-gifted self, you will want to submit and welcome more and more of God's solvent, scraping, sanding, and penetrating oil of love, knowing that you are being restored and renewed. Desire will grow, willingness will emerge, courage will rise, honesty will be easier, and trust in the God who loves you will undergird and strengthen you along this journey toward wholeness and soul restoration.

And, as I mentioned earlier, the journey of inner soul restoration is not a one-time passage, but a pilgrimage, "a long obedience in the same direction," as Eugene Peterson reminds us in his book of the same title.[16] Let's look now at what a true pilgrimage entails, and what postures will keep us moving steadily along the pathway to true inner soul restoration.

CHAPTER 2

The Posture of a Pilgrim

The gospel calls us to apprentice ourselves to Jesus, become pilgrims along the compassionate way, and journey deeper together into the heart and life of God.

—TREVOR HUDSON, *A MILE IN MY SHOES*

God is offering an invitation. . . . In the spiritual life, the long way around is the saving way. It isn't the quick and easy religion we are accustomed to. It's deep and difficult—a way that leads into the vortex of the soul where we touch God's transformative power.

—SUE MONK KIDD, *WHEN THE HEART WAITS*

Several years ago, Jeff and I participated in a service project to build playgrounds in the Czech Republic. We added a few days at the beginning of our trip to tour the city of Prague. With guidebook in hand, we took in as many sites as we could—from elaborate cathedrals to small points of interest, from the Charles Bridge to the Statue of Saint Wenceslas (from which some say the surname "Vancil" derived!). We were especially captivated by the Old Town Square with its display of history and architecture spanning eight centuries. The guidebook instructed us to walk around in a full circle, noting many different architectural styles from Romanesque to Gothic to Communist to Modern and others in between. We were enthusiastic tourists, taking a lot of pictures and absorbing all we could about this fascinating and beautiful city.

After we circled around the outer edges of the Old Town Square, our attention became riveted on the Jan Hus Monument in the middle. The main statue of Jan Hus was surrounded by figures of other people, some in warrior garb and others prostrate on the ground. The more we discovered about Jan Hus and the significance of his life and death, the more intrigued we became. He was a preacher of reformist ideas in the church and had many devoted followers throughout the Czech countryside. His primary passion focused on ensuring that the common folk had access to the teachings of Jesus and were allowed to participate in church regardless of their status. This was radically different from the predominant Roman Catholic traditions at the time. When asked to renounce his ideas, he refused, and was burned at the stake as a heretic on July 6, 1415. As the fire was about to start, he proclaimed, "In the same truth of the Gospel which I have written, taught, and preached . . . I am ready to die today." The monument honoring Hus and his followers was established in the middle of the Old Town Square five hundred years after his death, and July 6 is now a Czech national holiday. One inscription on the monument depicts his own words: LOVE EACH OTHER AND WISH THE TRUTH FOR EVERYONE.

The life of Jan Hus touched us deeply. Longing to know more, we found our way to the Bethlehem Chapel where he preached the truth of Jesus in the local language, so that everyone could understand it. The church was humble, simple, and austere, unlike the grand cathedrals we had already seen. I stepped through a narrow door onto a small platform where Hus once stood to preach. Tears filled my eyes as I realized I was standing at a place where my own encounter with God, centuries later, was made possible. Jan Hus's dedication, passion, and sacrifice were the foundations on which my experience of faith was able to stand; he fought and died to make the Scriptures accessible to common people like me. At that Holy Aha moment, I was no longer just a tourist, taking in sights. I was a pilgrim who had traveled to a sacred place where I felt a connection with the people who had lived long before me, those who shared my same yearning to know and follow Jesus in a deep and personal way.

If we had simply walked around the perimeter of the Old Town Square, following the instructions in the guidebook and pointing out the sites, we would have left Prague with good memories and an appreciation of the city, but we would have completely missed what God had for us to discover and experience—that inner holy "pilgrim" encounter that touched us and changed us.

I learned about the value and essence of being a pilgrim from our good friends Art and Janet, who completed a walking pilgrimage along the well-worn path of the Camino de Santiago in Spain. Their final destination was the shrine of the apostle Saint James the Great, located in the Cathedral of Santiago de Compostela. However, as is the case for all pilgrims, the personal impact of the journey happened along the way, not just when the destination was reached. Art and Janet shared some of what they learned from the experience: "Awareness comes to you with each step by embracing what is present in the moment." The slow pace, the power of silence, and traveling light gave them an openness to the sacred lessons found in their surroundings, like hearing roosters crow on the very day they had read about Peter's denial of Jesus. They gained an awakened sensitivity to the miracles of unexpected provisions, acts of kindness, and holy conversations between themselves and with others. The focus for each day was simple: get up, walk, and be present to what God had in store for them to see and discover. God spoke to both of them in powerful and personal ways, with words and images that were life-transforming.

One such image unfolded for Art on a day when he was walking by himself. At first, he envisioned his heart anchored to God's heart, and imagined the flow of love between them, back and forth, like the love between a parent and a child. The words of Hebrews 6:19–20 came alive for him: "We have this hope as an anchor for the soul, firm and secure. It enters the inner sanctuary behind the curtain, where Jesus has entered on our behalf." As the vision expanded, the image of God's love for him spread out like a giant sequoia tree, wide and broad and expansive, much larger than the love Art could ever express back to God. This sacred image became a lasting picture for Art of great intimacy and union with God, a "behind the curtain" experience of overwhelming divine love. Almost daily, Art taps into the "Sequoia love" of God as the anchor for his life and work.

When Art and Janet returned home, they adopted the motto "Camino-on in life." They shared with me some of their transformative takeaways: "God is always near and present." "We never lose connection with the Divine." "Slow down and listen." "See life through God's filter." "Enjoy God's creation more." The scripture from Acts 17:28 sums up what they learned experientially to be true: "For in him we live and move and have our being."

For many of us, taking a sojourn to a holy place somewhere else in the world isn't feasible or even on our bucket list. How then might we approach our lives with the "posture of a pilgrim" while also facing the ordinary and necessary demands of life? How do we "get up and walk" each day with an openness, attentiveness, and ability to see the holiness and healing available to us? How do we move from the outer edges of our existence to the sacred center of our lives in union with God?

One of my favorite books is Hannah Hurnard's *Hinds' Feet on High Places*. I had the privilege of meeting Ms. Hurnard near the end of her life. She was a woman of such humble and settled grace, the product of a lifelong journey with God and fifty years as a missionary in Palestine and Israel. *Hinds' Feet on High Places* is a captivating allegorical story that is an apt depiction of the raw and real experiences of a holy pilgrimage from fear to love, from frailty to strength, from bondage to freedom.

The main character of the story is Much-Afraid, who is feeble and timid. She is invited by the Shepherd, whom she loves and trusts, to go to the High Places, leaving the Valley of Humiliation where she is taunted by her Fearing relatives. She accepts the invitation and begins the trek with joyful anticipation that she'll soon be leaping effortlessly up the mountains and enjoying unlimited time with the Shepherd. However, her journey doesn't always go as she expected or hoped it would. For starters, she is accompanied by two sisters, Sorrow and Suffering, who are not exactly the companions she wanted or welcomed. The journey takes her to precipices, deserts, miles of loneliness, confrontations with enemies (like Bitterness, Pride, and Self-Pity), frightening darkness, glorious vistas, and eventually to a chasm where she surrenders her whole self. Along the way, she gathers stones to remind her of the lessons she learns. Regardless of what she encounters, Much-Afraid keeps going because she trusts the Shepherd and longs for the freedom and healing promised to her when she reaches the long-anticipated destination.

Finally, she arrives at the High Places—the Kingdom of Love—where her crippled feet are changed into hinds' feet and she is liberated from her persistent fears. She can now leap with freedom from one vista to another, learning from the Shepherd and taking in the grandeur of the mountainsides. She is renamed Grace and Glory, and her companions, the sisters, are changed into Joy and Peace. She also returns to the Valley of Humiliation to offer hope and love to the residents there, encouraging them to embark on the same journey to the High Places. One day, while talking with the Shepherd, she reviews her pilgrimage and recounts what she learned on her way to the High Places:

> *"First," she said, "I learned that I must accept with joy all that you allowed to happen to me on the way and everything to which the path led me. . . . Then I learned that I must bear all that others were allowed to do against me and to forgive with no trace of bitterness . . . that I may receive power to bring good out of this evil. The third thing I learned was that you, my Lord, never regarded me as I actually was, lame and weak and crooked and cowardly. You saw me as I would be when you had done what you promised and had brought me to the High Places. The fourth thing . . . was really the first thing I learned up here. Every circumstance in life, no matter how crooked and distorted and ugly it appears to be, if it is reacted to in love and forgiveness and obedience to your will can be transformed."*[1]

What glorious lessons and soul restoration Much-Afraid experienced in her transformation to Grace and Glory, the lasting results of maintaining the "posture of a pilgrim" every step along the way to the High Places, even when she was discouraged, doubtful, and disappointed. Gleaning from Art and Janet's experience and from Much-Afraid's journey to the High Places, I suggest four postures we can adopt when we respond to God's invitation to *come further in* along the journey toward freedom, healing, and inner soul restoration. *Slow down. Be expectant. Pay attention. Receive.*

Slow down. John Mark Comer, one of the salient voices among the new generation of biblical teachers, wrote a revolutionary, very practical, and timely book called *The Ruthless Elimination of Hurry: How to Stay Emotionally Healthy and Spiritually Alive in the Chaos of the Modern World*. Comer offers us so many poignant points about our need for a cure to what he calls "hurry sickness":

> "Hurry is the root problem underneath so many of the symptoms of toxicity in the world."

> "Not only does hurry keep us from the love, joy, and peace of the kingdom of God—the very core of what all human beings crave—but it also keeps us from God *himself* simply by stealing our attention. And with hurry, we always lose more than we gain."

> "Hurry is a form of violence for the soul."

> "The solution to an overbusy life is not more time. It's to slow down and simplify our lives around what really matters."[2]

Slowing down isn't easy to do in our fast-paced and full lives. We wake up, we do whatever duty requires of us and whatever we choose to do, and then we sleep. Minutes, hours, days, and years pass by, and we wonder, "Where did the time go?" Day after day we follow the script, often too tired, preoccupied, or oblivious to notice the sacred and significant moments and messages available right in front of us. We press on to get through one thing only to find ourselves getting through to the next thing. What if we slowed down more often, pausing to notice and savor the extraordinary moments and provisions in our ordinary lives? A child's laughter, a gentle breeze, a delicious meal, a kind cashier, a comfortable bed. What if we walked at the same pace God walked: the speed of love? This idea of God's pace comes from a passage in a book Art and Janet shared with me (which Comer also included in his own book): *Three Mile an Hour God*, by Kosuke Koyama:

> *God walks "slowly" because he is love. If he is not love he would have gone much faster. Love has its speed. It is an inner speed. It is a spiritual speed. It is a different kind of speed from the technological speed to which we are accustomed. It is "slow" yet it is lord over all other speed since it is the speed of love. It goes on in the depth of our life, whether we notice or not, whether we are currently hit by storm or not, at three miles an hour. It is the speed we walk and therefore it is the speed the love of God walks.*[3]

The greatest obstacle I face is my busy mind. The constant swirling of worries, ideas, responsibilities, and planning often keep me "hurried in my head" and unable to pause and be aware of God, myself, others, and my surroundings. Quite frankly, this often keeps me from truly enjoying my life. In his book *A Mile in My Shoes*, Trevor

Hudson describes what it means to be truly present in life: "Being present involves letting go of our constant preoccupations, immersing ourselves in the here and now, and giving ourselves wholeheartedly to whatever is at hand."[4] Yes! This is how I desire to live; it may not be easy or natural, but it inspires me to make slowing down a more conscious intention.

Be expectant. Are you ready and waiting for God to reveal something to you? A "pilgrim's posture" may involve intentional and helpful practices that expand our capacity to notice holy moments, like those offered by Christine Valters Paintner in *The Soul of a Pilgrim: Eight Practices for the Journey Within.*[5] And it can be as simple, and yet profound, as asking with anticipation a question I learned from Jamie and Donna Winship of Identity Exchange: *"God, what do You want me to see and know?"*[6] This can be a general inquiry about guidance for the day, or asked more specifically about a particular situation. Those who meet with me for spiritual direction will recognize this as one of the prominent questions I invite them to ask God when we're exploring a specific dilemma they face. Once asked, if you listen with expectancy, the One who wants to be known by you will show you, speak to you, or put an impression on your heart and mind. God's Spirit in union with your spirit will reveal holy thoughts and guidance. If you make conscious notes of what comes into your awareness, you will be ready and open to what God has for you to know and do. If you're looking with expectancy, you will see it.

Evelyn Underhill, in her book *The Spiritual Life,* describes the consequential outcome of waking up and ap-

proaching our lives with a holy expectancy to see what God
wants to show us:

> *When, for one reason or another, we begin to wake up*
> *a little bit, to lift the nose from the ground and notice*
> *the spiritual light and that spiritual atmosphere as*
> *real constituents of our human world; then, the*
> *whole situation is changed. Our horizon is widened,*
> *our experience is enormously enriched, and at the*
> *same time our responsibilities are enlarged. For now*
> *we get an entirely new idea of what human beings are*
> *for, and what they can achieve: and as a result, first*
> *our notions about life, our scale of values, begins to*
> *change, and then we do.*[7]

Pay attention. When we slow down and lean in with expectancy, we begin to notice the many ways God pursues us
and gets our attention—through people, nature, the Scriptures, an impression, a song, circumstances, discomfort,
conviction, and more. Have you had the experience of hearing the same theme or message a few days in a row—like
God is trying to tell you something specific? Frederick
Buechner encourages us with these words: "To love God
means to *pay attention,* be mindful, be open to the possibility that God is with you in ways that, unless you have your
eyes open, you may never glimpse. He speaks words that,
unless you have your ears open, you may never hear. Draw
near to him as best you can."[8]
One way God sometimes gets my attention is in my
nighttime dreams, perhaps because God knows it's a sure

way to get through to me when my mind isn't so distracted by the random details of my daily life. I often dream quite vividly, and most of the time the dreams disappear when I wake up. They usually don't make much sense anyway, and I'm often humored and baffled at who and what showed up during my nighttime slumber. Yet, sometimes a dream catches my attention, and I know there's a message in it, even if the specifics are jumbled and a bit obscure.

One such dream occurred during a season of prayerfully searching for more spiritual encouragement and community. In the dream I was boarding a train headed up a mountain for a day of skiing, something I love to do. Others were getting on the train, but were speaking in a language I didn't know. Afraid they'd find out I didn't belong there, I quickly tucked my ID in my back pocket, hiding my true identity. I nodded and smiled, pretending I understood what they were talking about. We reached a lookout spot and I saw a different mountain in the distance. It was all lit up with lots of colors outlining the numerous ski trails. My heart jumped and I knew that was the mountain for me! I headed back down the mountain to find my way there. When I woke up, the message from the dream was crystal clear: "Right desire. Wrong mountain!" In other words, my desire for spiritual nourishment and growth was right and good, but I was looking for it in places where people weren't speaking the language that resonated with my longings in that season of my life.

As a result, I decided to join a contemplative group I'd been considering. There I found a community of "spiritual skiers" who desired to experience God in much the same way I did, and this provided a place where I didn't need to "hide my ID." If I hadn't been leaning in with a posture to find "holy direction," I may have missed the impact of this nighttime message. I may have just been a tourist, dismissing the dream as silly and meaningless, rather than a pilgrim paying attention to a significant divine message.

Receive. The word *posture* implies a stance, an attitude, a direction one faces. Are you internally slumped over, bent by the burdens of life, closed and retracted with fear, doubt, anger, and shame, turned away from God, and therefore unreceptive to what's around you and how God might be speaking to you? Or are you turned toward God with an upright and open stance, praying, asking, and receptive to what is present for you to know and experience at any given moment?

Our pilgrimage to a more centered life with God requires receptivity to whatever God might reveal to us, whether it's something uplifting to embrace or difficult to accept. Like Much-Afraid, we may be accompanied by sorrow and suffering and we will likely encounter difficulties, doubts, disruptions, discouragements, and disappointments. Yet, also like Much-Afraid, if we're willing to receive all that God has for us in our everyday lives, we can enjoy life on the High Places with glorious freedom and unlimited awareness of God's love and presence. As we're reminded in Ephesians 1:3, God "has blessed us in the heavenly realms with every spiritual blessing in Christ." May we receive, with deep gratitude, the fullness of all this means.

While I was attending a retreat with a group of spiritual directors, the morning speaker encouraged us to engage more intentionally and prayerfully with what is right in front of us in our everyday lives. She then invited us to spend the afternoon in silence, walking the grounds and receiving what God might show us through nature, through the quiet, and in our own hearts. We were also invited to create something to share with the group during our evening time together. I wrote the following poem, titled "Two Walks," during my time of reflection as I became aware of two postures I can walk in my life: closed or open.

Two Walks

Closed	Open
Head down	Head raised
Eyes on the gravel	Eyes alert
Hurried steps	Slow steps on the gravel
Mind is full	Curious mind
Scattered thoughts	Settled
So much to do	Heart awake
Worried	Noticing
Tightened chest	Mirrored images on the lake
Shoulders hunched	Puffs of white on spindly branches
Heart asleep	Tall trunks reaching upward
Blinders on	Reflective others strolling by
Not noticing	Textures of decaying logs
Alone.	Hovering hillsides lined with trees
	Surrounded within a circle of God's messengers
	Inviting me in as one of their own.

—MARILYN VANCIL, JANUARY 2019

As I mentioned earlier, I participated in a contemplative community when I was seeking more spiritual support for my life. My first experience was a ten-month course with Selah Center called Living From The Heart.[9] During the first gathering, we reflected on an allegorical story called "The Carpenter and the Unbuilder" by David M. Griebner. It's the tale of a man, the Carpenter, who lived in a certain kingdom and was invited to come and dine with the king. After carefully preparing for the pilgrimage to the castle, the man set out. Along the way, he stopped and built several shelters to stay in. At first he intended to stay only for a short time, but ended up improving the buildings and living in them for long periods of time, often forgetting about the king's invitation. One day, another traveler, named the Unbuilder, stopped by and reminded the Carpenter of the dinner invitation, encouraging him to "unbuild" so that his journey to the anticipated meal with the king could continue. The Carpenter agreed to continue on with the Unbuilder the next day. When the Carpenter invited the Unbuilder to stay in the home with him for the night, the Unbuilder declined and remarked, "*It is easier to notice the wonderful things the king has put along the way when you aren't looking out from inside something you have built to protect yourself.*"[10] The next day, the Carpenter resumed his journey to the king, but not without stopping several times to build more structures. "*In the meantime the king kept the food warm, which he was very good at doing.*"[11]

The gracious and relentless invitation to "come and dine with the king" never expires. The pilgrimage of our lives toward the full realization of the spiritual feast available to us is one day at a time, one step at a time—as Art and Janet stated so well: "to get up, walk, and be present to what God has for you." The "posture of a pilgrim" on the journey toward a more centered life with God means slowing down, being expectant, paying attention, and receiving. And, like the Carpenter, we will pass through some stops on our pilgrimage, what I call Signposts Along the Way. Let's look now at some of those markers on our spiritual path.

CHAPTER 3

Signposts Along the Way

Let us throw off everything that hinders and the sin that so easily entangles. And let us run with perseverance the race marked out for us, fixing our eyes on Jesus, the pioneer and perfecter of faith.

—HEBREWS 12:1–2

We have spent our own energy; we have come to the end of our ropes. We are ready to learn about freedom—the liberty of living without grasping. At the same time that we surrender our wills to be healed spiritually, we simultaneously begin to be healed psychologically. The healing itself is mysterious and profound, for it is the soul that is healed.

—JANET O. HAGBERG AND ROBERT A. GUELICH,
THE CRITICAL JOURNEY

I began to meet with Claire for spiritual direction at a time when she was seeking a more connected life with God while also grappling with what she truly believed. Her spiritual journey started at a very young age; she felt drawn like a magnet to all things related to God and decided on her own to attend a local Jesus-centered church. She longed to learn all she could about the wondrous God who had captured her attention. Claire adhered wholeheartedly to the doctrinal beliefs she was taught and enjoyed the companionship of other like-minded believers. Her faith at that time was "full of gusto" with a focused mission and purpose. Later, in her college and early career years, Claire began to question her faith when she realized how the rigid beliefs and defined roles of her church experience had resulted in restrictions and judgments on herself and others. She was confused as to how the story she had thought to be true about Jesus made sense in the expanded world she had come to know and care about. The doctrinal "plumb line" by which she had previously measured her faith was no longer acceptable, leaving her unsettled and full of questions. Her longing for intimacy with God never wavered, but she wasn't sure how to have an authentic faith while also discounting some of her former beliefs. Around this same time, she was introduced to the Enneagram, which gave her a better understanding of her internal life and presented her with a desirable path of growth. This motivated Claire to contact me to discuss her Enneagram pattern and her changing spirituality. Throughout our first two years together, we discussed the Enneagram a bit, but we mostly explored her sincere and thoughtful quest to understand and experience God in a real and meaningful way.

During a time of transition, Claire also suffered a deeply personal and disappointing loss. In her raw grief, she felt the physical presence of God—like a personal hug—in a way she hadn't in a very long time. She sensed God assuring her that *I'm not out there; I'm here*. She noticed a settling peace inside and felt a freshness in her life with God, similar to moving to a new vista point on a long hike. She shared with me how she now felt able and relieved to honor both spaces for herself with honesty and authenticity—to believe and follow Jesus as a foundation for her life and to also question and explore more about God so that her understanding and experience could expand. For Claire, the "plumb line" changed from doctrinal alignment to one of Love and Goodness with "more trust in my connection with God in me and accepting that God is bigger and more mysterious than I will ever grasp."

Claire's journey of faith, and that of many others who meet with me for spiritual direction, corresponds closely to the spiritual journey described by Janet Hagberg and Robert Guelich in their book *The Critical Journey: Stages in the Life of Faith*. When I first learned about these stages of faith, I could relate to all of the stages and was relieved to realize my own faith experiences, especially the seasons of questions and introspection, were normal and "right on track." When I explain these stages to others, they feel comforted and affirmed, knowing they are on a common, though sometimes disquieting, path of spiritual pilgrimage.

Following is a brief summary of the stages of faith as presented by Hagberg and Guelich, using direct quotes from their book.[1]

As with any attempt to describe the mysterious relationship between the divine and the human, the categorization of stages risks the danger of reducing the spiritual journey to prescriptive steps. This is not the intent of the authors, nor mine, in sharing this paradigm of the faith pilgrimage. I offer this here for two primary reasons. One is to provide you with some signposts along the way for your faith journey, giving you hope and inspiration to keep pursuing intimacy with God, even when times are dark or you're not sure what you believe or where you stand.

The second reason for listing these stages of faith is to highlight how the exploration and use of the Enneagram often follows a similar path. I'm going to make a bold statement here: *The value of the Enneagram will lessen and become less relevant and applicable the closer you abide in the center space with God.* You may be surprised that an Enneagram aficionado like myself would admit such a reality. Yet we need to recognize when the Enneagram is a useful tool and when it's less so. This is a significant point to consider, and I'll cover it further in the following chapter.

As you read through each stage, consider your own faith journey and what rings true for you. Remember that all of these stages—the Recognition of God, the Discipleship Life, the Productive Life, the Journey Inward, the Wall, the Journey Outward, and the Life of Love—are equally significant and valuable. As Hagberg and Guelich explain in their opening chapters, the stages are more like a spiral, and we may go back and forth between stages or experience more than one at a time. They are not static, and not everyone's journey is the same. Although they seem sequential, they are more cyclical and cumulative, building on one another. This doesn't mean that those at later stages are better or spiritually superior to those in the earlier stages.[2]

Stage 1: The Recognition of God

Stage 1, the recognition of God, is where we all begin the journey of faith. We may experience it during early childhood or as adults who come for the first time to recognize the reality or presence of Someone who stands behind it all. Regardless of our age, however, it seems true that most begin the journey in a childlike way. We come to it with an innocence, a freshness, that is seldom ever again as vivid or vital. . . . It is accepting the fact of the reality of God in our lives. This is a very simple, though not always easy, act. It requires no study or prerequisites. Frequently, it happens very naturally. We simply know that God is there. . . . Whatever route leads us to begin the spiritual journey, awe most likely underlies it at some point.[3]

When did you first know there was a God, that there was Someone who stands behind it all? Perhaps you don't even remember a time when God wasn't real to you, or perhaps you can recall a specific moment when you knew for sure that there is a God. Although I went to church with my family as a child, it wasn't until I learned that I could know Jesus personally that I responded with a new sense of belief. So, I raised my hand at church camp when I was twelve. At the time, I was also motivated to avoid hell, which I heard was a possibility! Regardless of how little I knew and whether or not the teachings were correct, I just knew God was real and close to me. I also had similar moments of spiritual "awe" about the reality of God through my involvement in Young Life during high school and college. I also witnessed Stage 1 "awes" for others during the thirty-five years Jeff and I served with this nonprofit outreach ministry. The fresh realization that there was a God who knew and loved them was a wonder to behold in the lives of countless youth.

Stage 2: The Discipleship Life

This stage is best characterized as a time of learning and belonging. . . . Stage 2 frees us to explore, to learn, to quest, to absorb, to put into place our set of beliefs or faith principles. In this stage, we learn the most about God as perceived by others we respect and trust. We are apprentices. It is a time to be with other people in that process, a social time with companion searchers on the journey. . . . This is a taking stage, a filling stage. . . . We learn to be obedient disciples. . . . At this stage people see the cause or leader as the answer because it has truly enlightened or changed them. They become enthusiastic to see others have the same experience so they too can find satisfaction.[4]

Notebook in hand, pen ready, Bible open, and a heart to learn. Fresh Holy Ahas come readily when we eagerly absorb as much as we can about our faith in God during Stage 2. I'm beyond grateful for the many opportunities I had to learn and grow and for the people who inspired me—they all established a solid foundation for my understanding of the Scriptures and God's principles. Without these, I'm sure I would have floundered and become like the seeds that fell on the path and were snatched away, or on the rocky soil with no roots, or among the thorns choked out by the cares of the world (Matthew 13). Although I can look back and see, like Claire, that some of what I learned was limiting and not the full picture of God's grace, at least I had a "table to push against," as Paula D'Arcy expresses in a CD series with Richard Rohr called *A Spirituality for the Two Halves of Life*. What she meant by this phrase is that her early understanding of the Catholic catechism, which was often taught around their family dinner table, provided a solid foundation for the agonizing questions and doubts about God when her life was upended by the tragic death of her husband and child.[5]

Stage 3: The Productive Life

Stage 3 is best described as the "doing" stage. It is the period of time when we most consciously find ourselves working for God. In fact, our faith is characterized as just that, working for God or being in God's service. . . . This usually is a very active phase on the

> *critical journey. It is positive and dynamic, centered on being productive in the area of our faith. It nourishes us because it is so personally rewarding, even when the objective is to help others. . . . For many, this stage describes the height of their faith experience. It feels exciting, fulfilling, awesome, inspiring, fruitful.*[6]

This stage is when your faith informs how to live your life in the context of your circumstances—in your relationships, your work, and your community. For Jeff and me, during these "productive" years, our faith and understanding of God's ways influenced how we raised our children, how we used our time and money, who we hung out with, and how we served in our communities and churches. We were active, we were dedicated, we were engaged, and we were purposeful in what we did. We're so grateful for how we grew from the opportunities we were given, for the amazing people who enriched our lives in countless ways, and for how God used us to encourage others in their growing faith. As said above, this season is usually rewarding, exciting, and fruitful. It certainly was for us!

Stages 4, 5, 6, and the Wall: The Inner Healing Stages

Stages 4 through 6 represent a difficult personal transformation and reemerging that require a rediscovery on a different level of what faith and spirituality are all about. These are the inner healing stages (spiritually and psychologically) for which the journey cannot be prescribed.[7]

Based on my own personal experience, when I was catapulted into the unfamiliar territory of questioning and rejecting some of what I had previously believed about God and Jesus, I didn't know what was really happening inside of me. I felt confused and alone, like bobbing in a rubber raft out in the ocean, hoping for a rescue but with no lifeline in sight. I was also concerned that I might be "going over the edge" with some of the new thoughts about God I was entertaining. So, as I said before, when I heard about the following stages and recognized my own experience in what Hagberg and Guelich described, I breathed a sigh of relief and felt courage and hope to keep pursuing God, even in the unsettledness. I trust this offers the same encouragement for you.

For some of you, especially the younger set, the following stages may not make any sense or resonate with your life at all. You may also hope to avoid Stage 4 and the Wall, and wish you knew how to skip through them and just move on to Stages 5 and 6. Some people resist moving forward at all or will push their struggles out of their awareness, content to remain in the comfortable and familiar patterns and beliefs established in earlier stages. I'm telling you now, if you're serious about your life with God and are open and paying attention, it's highly likely that someday you will hit what Hagberg and Guelich call the Wall and it will throw you for a "spiritual loop." This may happen when you face a crisis or when you internally sense an unsettling shift or spiritual restlessness. When that happens, I hope you'll recall what you've learned here—that this turning point is a common and critical part of God's invitation to *come further in.*

Stage 4: The Journey Inward

Stage 4, The Journey Inward, is aptly described by its title for it is a deep and very personal inward journey. It almost always comes as an unsettling experience yet results in healing for those who continue through it. . . . It's a mode of questioning, exploring, falling apart, doubting, dancing around the real issues, sinking into uncertainty, and indulging in self-centeredness. . . . It becomes painfully clear, after some initial squirming in another attempt to be comfortable, that the right direction rather than the right answers have to come from God. That realization generally comes through a deep inner journey . . . one that we are not informed or taught about and for which there are few models available. . . . When this stage comes, many feel propelled into it by an event outside themselves. It's usually a crisis that turns their world upside down. . . . For the first time, our faith does not seem to work. . . . Our formula of faith,

*whatever that may have been, does not work any-
more, or so it appears. We are stumped, hurting,
angry, betrayed, abandoned, unheard, or unloved. . . .
Stage 4 allows us, invites us, and compels us to know
ourselves and to know God in all God's fullness. We
may experience a complete turnabout in our concept
of both ourselves and God. This often comes through
a slow process.*[8]

Stage 4 is a time of introspection. This may feel wrong, he-
retical, and overly self-absorbed. After all, aren't we followers of Jesus supposed to deny ourselves and serve God
rather than "navel gaze"? It may seem as if you're abandon-
ing your call to service, the needs of others, or the foundations of your faith altogether. And confusion about who
and what to believe can send your faith in a tailspin. Take
heart. The time to contemplate your inner life with all its
questions, longings, and explorations of your faith will
lead you further toward a more centered life with God. Entering this stage is also imperative for the process of inner
soul restoration.

"Deconstruction" is a popular word thrown around to
describe what is, perhaps, a Stage 4 passageway in a person's experience with God, Jesus, faith, church, and the
Scriptures. Is this the best word? I wonder. I observe people
stuck in dismantling and rejecting their former faith, criticizing and blaming the church and others for how their former faith experiences failed them, expected too much of
them, didn't live up to the promises, didn't make them

happy, or are no longer relevant or meaningful. The end result can be a loss of connection and interest in God altogether. Exploring the impact of one's spiritual background is very important and a crucial part of the Stage 4 season; we need to "unbuild" some of our past experiences and beliefs, and honestly address any injuries and injustices we've suffered from religious institutions and spiritual leaders. But does it help a person to move on from the past if they lose their longing for God altogether by remaining stuck in their disappointment, disillusionment, and anger?

I'm wondering if perhaps a better, more forward-thinking consideration is to reframe this season of questioning and disruption as an invitation to echo the apostle Paul's words: "But one thing I do: Forgetting what is behind and straining toward what is ahead, I press on toward the goal to win the prize for which God has called me heavenward in Christ Jesus" (Philippians 3:13–14). In the preceding verses, Paul deems his former religious fervor and accolades as "rubbish" (NKJV). Think about rubbish: it's something that once had value and purpose, but is no longer useful or functional. Paul calls out the rigors and fallacies of his previous religious life, but he doesn't stay there bemoaning them. He lets go of his past and presses on to God's higher purposes in Jesus for him. In the confusion and muddle of Stage 4, this pathway may not seem so clear or easy, but seeing it as an invitation for spiritual deepening rather than a deconstruction project might elicit more hope and courage for those who find themselves in this season of inner upheaval.

The Wall

Somewhere toward the end of Stage 4 we experience the Wall; a face-to-face experience with God and with our own will. . . . The Wall represents the place where another layer of transformation occurs and a new life of faith begins for those who feel called and have the courage to move into it. . . . The process of meeting the Wall requires going through the Wall, not underneath it, over it, around it, or blasting it. We must go through brick by brick, feeling and healing each element of our wills as we surrender to God's will. . . . We move toward wholeness and holiness. . . . Doubtless it is apparent now that we cannot go through the Wall by ourselves. We need God to lead us; otherwise our will would be in charge. Even approaching the Wall is uncomfortable because we feel both a pending loss and a great longing for new life, healing, or meaning. We bring anticipation and dread. . . . Mystery lies at the core of the Wall; a mystery ultimately defies explanation but includes discomfort, surrender, healing, awareness, forgiveness, acceptance, love, closeness to God, discernment, melting, molding, and solitude and reflection.[9]

Going through the Wall includes a large variety of conflicting feelings. Some are appealing, like anticipation, and others the opposite, like dread. Sifting through the above explanation of the Wall, the phrase that captures the essence of this stage, in my opinion, is "healing each element of our wills as we surrender to God's will." Oh no. Surrender. Does it really have to come to *that*?

David Benner, in his book *Surrender to Love: Discovering the Heart of Christian Spirituality,* wrote a brilliant chapter on surrender and obedience. I wish I could copy and paste the whole thing; I underlined most of it. Benner tackles the difficult and often misunderstood implication of these two words, "surrender" and "obedience," and their vital place in experiencing the true freedom our hearts long to know. What he states emphatically is that surrender to God makes sense only if you know and trust God's unconditional and lasting love.

> *Surrender is the foundational dynamic of Christian freedom—surrender of my efforts to live my life outside of the grasp of God's love and surrender to God's will and gracious Spirit. . . . It is a readiness to trust that is based on love. . . . Surrender to God flows out of the experience of love that will never let me go. It is the response of the heart that knows that since God is for me, nothing can come between me and the perfect love that surrounds me and will support me regardless of my effort, my response or even my attention.*[10]

The process of surrendering our "ego will" to God is like a climber gripping the side of a cliff in desperation. With knuckles bent and shaking, the climber hangs on for dear life, fearful of falling into a deep abyss of unknown depth and likely peril. I can only guess at the two main reasons a climber would let go. One is absolute exhaustion and loss of strength, making it impossible to hold on any longer. The other is having faith in a companion climber who has them securely belayed to a solid structure and will catch them once they release their grip, thus leading to an exhilarating experience of free-falling and freedom. Avid rock climbers keep going back for more of this; apparently there's nothing quite like the sensation of dropping into thin air and eventually being caught. For me personally, it sounds terrifying.

The reasons a rock climber would release a tight grip are similar to those for surrendering our will to God's loving will. Because the survival strategies of our ego-centered Adapted Selves have been a part of our way of living for such a long time, it's hard to let go, not knowing what we'll be like without them. We fear falling into an emotional abyss where we don't know who we are or how to live. Yet, when we come to the end of our own strength and abilities, we realize we have no option but to finally give up and give in. It's a bit unnerving, but we'll soon discover that we're hooked securely to "God's belay" and that we will be caught by God's holy love for us. Letting go and free-falling into God's love and will is nothing like any other human experience—bringing with it greater freedom, inner restoration, and a renewed awareness of never being alone.

Henri Nouwen's words sum up the invitation of the Wall and surrender to God: "Jesus says, 'Let go of your complaints, forgive those who loved you poorly, step over your feelings of being rejected, and have the courage to trust that you won't fall into an abyss of nothingness but into the safe embrace of a God whose love will heal all your wounds.' "[11]

Stage 5: The Journey Outward

Now we surrender to God's will to fully direct our lives, but with our eyes wide open, aware but unafraid of the consequences. Once parts of the deep, excruciating inward journey have been experienced, the natural outcome is to venture outside of one's self-centeredness and back into the active world with a new sense of fulfillment . . . based on the growth and peace of mind we have experienced from the inner journey. . . . The movement of Stage 5 is on the horizontal, the outward, reaching out to other people from a sense of fullness, of being loved by God, and being asked to love others in return. It is such a natural process that we hardly recognize it is happening. Our hearts are different, and our lives evolve from that change. . . . At this point in the journey, we let God be God from the inside out instead of the outside in. We let God direct our lives from a calm stillness inside, from a peace of soul and mind.[12]

One of my favorite slides in my presentation on the Enneagram is a four-part cartoon I found on the internet. In the first frame, a seed is nicely tucked in the dark dirt with a thought bubble that reads, "Ah, this is the life. I could stay here forever!" The second frame shows the outer seed coat starting to peel away, and the bubble reads, "Wait . . . what's happening to me?" In the third frame, the seed coat is pulling away even more. "Oh God!! The pain!! Kill me now!" And the final frame is a new green sprout above the ground saying, "Huh?" These four frames capture the movement from our Adapted Self ways of being to the glorious growth of our Authentic Self, like the peeling away of the seed coat so that the true seed can flourish and be fruitful.

The last frame describes Stage 5—we experience a surprise, a wonder, a settled peace, a new perspective, less striving, more acceptance, and the emergence of greater love without strings. It just starts to happen! Life with God becomes deeper and more authentic, with less effort to maintain the connection. We know we've changed, and we know it's not a result of a new self-improvement plan we've adopted. New sprouts of grace, love, hope, contentment, generosity, courage, joy, tenderness, and engagement start to grow internally, and are expressed externally. We move outward to serve God and love others with a new ease and commitment. Here we gratefully say, "Thank You, God, for Your wondrous works."

Our family was fortunate to spend many summers at a camp located at the mouth of a stunning five-mile fjord in Canada. A narrow fifty-yard channel alongside the camp connected the open seas to the peaceful waters of the inlet. Rapids both in and out were created when the tides changed. Many yachts would travel through this channel on their way to the majestic waterfalls at the end of the fjord. Wise skippers would wait until the water was flowing in, making their journey through the passageway relatively easy. Impatient and overly confident skippers would sometimes try to enter the channel against the current, thinking they could fight their way through to the other side. It rarely worked and was quite dangerous; to avoid crashing on the rocks, they usually had to give up and turn back to wait until the tide had shifted.

God's will and our wills can flow together in the same direction toward the wonder and glory of all God has for us. Once we stop fighting for our own will to prevail, we join the movement of the Spirit in and through our lives and we no longer need to strive as much to be perfect, needed, successful, special, self-sufficient, certain, happy, strong, and settled. Instead, we embody those attributes more and more. We live with less internal angst and with more enjoyment of the wonders that surround us. We live more fully and freely as God's treasures in the center of Divine Love.

Stage 6: The Life of Love

At this stage, we reflect God to others in the world more clearly and consistently than we ever thought possible. . . . When we are at Stage 6, we have lost ourselves in the equation, and at the same time we have truly found ourselves. . . . We are at peace with ourselves, fully conscious of being the person God created us to be. . . . We can live openly and vulnerably with others, because we do not need self-protection . . . our lives are permeated with un-conditional love. . . . We are like vessels into which God pours His Spirit, constantly overflowing. We are Spirit-filled but in a quiet, unassuming way. . . . When at Stage 6 we still experience pain or shock, it tires or angers us, but we can also simultaneously experience God's grace, humor, and comfort in the midst of it all. We do not fear pain, trauma, disappointments, or even death, because God is there to provide and lead us on. . . . We experience life itself as both a gift and a miracle. . . . We are free of encumbrances. We travel light. . . . This stage represents not our work, our calling, our life, but the life we live in God. It is all about the transcendent life we live beyond ourselves but rooted in God.[13]

What a beautiful description of a centered life with God! Oh, don't you wish you could just sail into the Life of Love without having to pass through the murky waters and rough seas of Stage 4 and the Wall? I don't think it's possible; what we experience and learn in those passages will carry us through to the quiet harbors of Stages 5 and 6. The word that comes to mind when I read through the description of Stage 6 is "freedom." Freedom from fear, anger, and shame. Freedom from striving. Freedom to love. Freedom to forgive. Freedom to trust. Freedom to rest. Freedom to be restored.

Oh, the glories of union with God, the One who loves you, knows you, guides you, and abides in you by the Spirit! May you hold this holy destination always before you, no matter which signpost you are passing by. Your sacred pilgrimage from the outside edges of your Adapted Self patterns to the holy center of your Authentic Self in union with God, the inner harbor of grandeur and depth, is your divine destiny!

CHAPTER 4

Stages on the Enneagram Journey

It is no surprise to me that the Enneagram is so distasteful to soft spirituality and even to individualistic spirituality. The Enneagram does not disguise the pain, the major surgery, or the price of enlightenment.

—RICHARD ROHR, *THE ENNEAGRAM:*
A CHRISTIAN PERSPECTIVE

Because our Adapted Self and our Authentic Self are not packed in two separate, clearly labeled boxes, we have trouble discerning which parts of ourselves to disown in order to enjoy the freedom of living out our divine destiny and finding our true selves in God. That's the gift of the Enneagram.

—*SELF TO LOSE, SELF TO FIND*

propose that one's experience with the Enneagram follows a path similar to the stages of faith just described in the previous chapter. Please keep in mind I'm not equating one's experience of the Enneagram with the sacred and holy pilgrimage of one's life with God. The Enneagram can be a useful instrument along the pathway toward a centered life with God, but it is *not* the golden key that will unlock life's complexities, solve the mysteries of your human experience, or make certain that you have a more vibrant spiritual life. A danger exists in putting too much emphasis and credence on the Enneagram, and it can become, in many ways, a form of idolatry. Jesus warned about this kind of mindset when He confronted some religious leaders who challenged Him. "You study the Scriptures diligently because you think that in them you have eternal life. These are the very Scriptures that testify about me, yet you refuse to come to me to have life" (John 5:39–40). A twist on this might read, "You study the Enneagram diligently because you think it will bring you life, but you don't come to Me to find the life you are looking for."

That said, don't get me wrong! I think the Enneagram is one of the most helpful and dynamic tools for self-discovery, awareness, and growth. It provides valuable insights into the human personality better than any other assessment I know, and I will continue to teach it and utilize it personally and professionally. But I will also include the additional perspective of *The Drawing,* which I'll explain in the next section. I believe this fresh paradigm will enhance one's spiritual pilgrimage beyond what the traditional Enneagram model offers.

In *Self to Lose, Self to Find,* I shared four words that describe how using the Enneagram has impacted my own life: *comfort, compassion, confession,* and *consent.* These line up with how the stages of the Enneagram journey unfold for many people. Maybe you will see your own experience reflected in the following four stages of the Enneagram experience:

Stage 1: Recognition of Self on the Enneagram: Comfort

An initial introduction to the Enneagram feels invigorating and exciting, like a Holy Aha moment that brings clarity and enlightenment. A common response after discovering one's dominant type is "Wow, this is so great, so interesting, so amazing!" New and refreshing self-recognition opens up, like a light turning on and illuminating one's unique way of being in the world. Fascination, intrigue, and relief are common feelings. It's comforting to know there are identifiable reasons for how and why you think, act, and feel as you do. It's a comfort to be understood and accepted for who you are and how you live. Even if you can't quite identify your type, knowing there's a tool to better understand yourself offers relief while also building a curiosity to uncover more insights about who you are and how you operate in life.

It's also a great comfort to recognize, as I proposed in *Self to Lose, Self to Find,* that each Enneagram type reflects attributes of God, and that *you* were created to experience and express divine qualities in a unique way, as your Authentic Self. When the Enneagram types are understood like this—as mirrors of the Divine: Goodness (1), Love (2), Hope (3), Depth (4), Wisdom (5), Faithfulness (6), Joy (7), Power (8), and Peace (9)—it's awe-inspiring and comforting to realize there's a holy purpose for your life.

Stage 2: Learning About the Enneagram: Compassion

If you become engaged with the Enneagram, the next stage is all about learning more and soaking up information: reading books, listening to podcasts, seeking out experts, attending workshops, asking questions, and trying to understand all the nuances of this personality system. You learn about the arrows, wings, subtypes, harmony triads, social styles, and more. You also enjoy talking about it with other people, engaging in lively conversations, finding out their types, and sharing personal stories. At some point, you may become obsessed with the Enneagram, searching for that one explanation that captures everything about you. If you take in too much information, you may become more confused about your type because you can generally find something in each type description that resonates with your life in some way. You're also tempted to label other people so you can understand and interact with them better. Along with this, you become an "Enneagram evangelist," sharing books or suggesting podcasts so others in your life will come on board and join in your enthusiasm.

As you learn more about the Enneagram, you become painfully aware of the weaknesses, compulsive habits, unattractive reactions, strivings, and internal obstacles that keep you stuck in repeating patterns you don't really like. You begin to recognize the internal accusing voices that make you feel that you're not worthy, you're unlovable, you're not valued, you're deficient, you're inadequate, you're incapable, you're not enough, you're too much, you're insignificant. You also see that others suffer from similar struggles. This emerging awareness presents an opportunity to grow in compassion, acceptance, and non-judgment for yourself and others, realizing that everyone is like a "damaged chair in the garage" with an accumulation of experiences, perceptions, injuries, choices, rewards, and motivations. Love, grace, and forgiveness are important divine qualities to be accessed and expressed toward yourself and others during this learning stage and beyond.

Stage 3: Using the Enneagram Productively: Confession

The next phase is a time of discovering how the Enneagram knowledge you've obtained can direct you to becoming a healthier and more balanced person. The arrows—often called the paths of integration and disintegration—give you clues about persistent reactions to stress and potential practices for growth so you can develop new strategies in your everyday life. The Enneagram will reveal dynamics in your relationships, hopefully to foster more honest and open communication about misunderstandings and conflicts, as well as greater acceptance and appreciation for others in your life. Once you know the gifts and challenges of your particular type, this knowledge can guide you in offering your time and talents and how to become more effective and productive in your work and calling.

As your awareness increases about the Enneagram and the nuances of your particular pattern, you'll notice your self-orientation, self-protection, and baffling behaviors more and more. And you will get tired of them! You may strive to change, but the ingrained beliefs and subconscious motivations are difficult to work on with much lasting success. Honest and humble confession of resentment, pride, deceit, envy, greed, anxiety, insatiability, shamelessness, and indolence will turn you toward God for forgiveness and release from these traps. This confession will set you free to more fully reclaim the Authentic Self you were created to be and the true self you long to be. As 1 John 1:9 reminds us, "If we confess our sins, he is faithful and just and will forgive us our sins and purify us from all unrighteousness."

Stages 4, 5, 6: The Enneagram Hits the Wall: Consent

Through these later stages, the Enneagram ceases to be as helpful or insightful as it was initially. It may still be a reference point, a way to articulate what you're feeling and thinking. But one thing is certain: for the Enneagram to be truly transformative, *it must lead you to the Wall,* where you are completely convinced you're trapped and can't change on your own! At this point, knowing and revealing your Enneagram type should no longer be entertaining; it should become humiliating and you should feel hopeless.

When both Jeff and I hit our "Enneagram Wall" (several times actually), it launched us into a deeper awareness of our need for God and the impossibility of changing ourselves. For a long time I thought it was pretty nice to be a Nine. That is, until my sweet hospitable self was no longer happy and easygoing. I got tired of being indecisive, tossed to and fro, unfocused, and dependent on others to direct my life. I remember shouting in exasperation, "I hate being a Nine!" Poring over the latest Enneagram book affirmed my sorry state, but learning more didn't dissolve my pain or angst.

When Jeff became painfully aware of how trapped he was in the vortex of his Type Three patterns, he felt humiliated and sorrowful. He realized he had always been able to repent of various behaviors and attitudes, but he felt hopeless when he recognized how deeply seated the false narratives of a Three were within him. He cried out, "Oh Lord, how do I repent from *who* I am?" Romans 7:24 echoed Jeff's own thoughts: "What a wretched man I am! Who will rescue me from this body that is subject to death?" We both learned the reality that the only way forward was honest confession and consent to God's restorative work within us.

The best hope—the only hope—for transformation and release from the habitual patterns of our Adapted Self is to surrender to God's redeeming and persistent love. We get through the Wall by the presence, guidance, and wisdom of the Spirit, not by becoming experts on the Enneagram. You can even leave the Enneagram behind. Although you'll always be influenced and tempted by your dominant Enneagram pattern, it will no longer describe you, because your Enneagram type is not your true, God-gifted identity.

Many people at my Enneagram workshops who are of the "older" set, and who have walked with Jesus for a long time, will say they don't recognize themselves in any of the nine different types. They often comment that they used to be like one of the types when they were younger, but not anymore. Why? Because it's the redeeming power of God's Spirit that transforms us from our Adapted Self existence to our Authentic Self living, from the traps of our survival strategies to freedom in the center of our life with God. The Enneagram is a helpful tool for our spiritual journey, useful as we pass through some stages of our faith development, but its value is quite limited for going through the Wall and on to the later stages of our spiritual pilgrimage. As M. Robert Mulholland Jr. puts it, "God is one who, in the very essence of God's being, comes to us in our false self, who enters into our false self to liberate us from its destructive bondage from which we cannot liberate ourselves, and to enable us to be restored in the fullness of God's very own image in loving union with God."[1] My addition to this statement would be "The Enneagram cannot liberate us either."

Comfort. Compassion. Confession. Consent. These are signposts along the Enneagram journey, but God's invitation to *come further in* will take us beyond what the Enneagram can ever offer. There will come a time when we can set it aside and lean into the redeeming and restorative work of God in our lives.

Let's review what we've covered so far in Section I before we move on to Section II and my introduction of *The Drawing*. In Chapter 1, we explored what inner soul restoration means and involves, including *desire*, *willingness*, *courage*, *honesty*, and, of greatest importance, *trust* in the One who alone can reclaim the one-of-a-kind masterpiece of our Authentic Self. Chapter 2 reminded us that this journey toward wholeness and restoration is a long pilgrimage, requiring the posture of a pilgrim who *slows down*, *expects*, *pays attention*, and *receives*. In Chapter 3, you learned the stages of faith that serve as signposts along the way. And lastly, in Chapter 4, we reviewed the stages of the Enneagram journey, recognizing that this tool will become less helpful along one's pilgrimage toward a centered life with God.

Now that you know these foundations for comprehending the fresh paradigm I'm introducing, I present to you *The Drawing*, beginning with an explanation of two possible perspectives for engaging with tools like the Enneagram.

SECTION II

The Drawing:
A Fresh Paradigm

Something's trying to emerge. . . . Let yourself be drawn by a different voice. . . . Something's trying to make its presence known. . . . Imagine not being afraid. . . . Imagine not resisting the greater power. . . . Something is moving, pressing through your circumstances. . . . Imagine how you would grow if you listened.

—PAULA D'ARCY, *SEEKING WITH ALL MY HEART: ENCOUNTERING GOD'S PRESENCE TODAY*

CHAPTER 5

Bounded Set and Centered Set Perspectives

Any tool or concept that reduces a person to a label or type without a deep dive into their context and their open range for development is missing half the point.

—ROB MCKENNA, PH.D., "YOU'RE MORE THAN
A NUMBER AND TYPE"

You are a whole person who has a whole identity—you are all nine numbers.

—DR. JEROME D. LUBBE, *THE BRAIN-BASED ENNEAGRAM:
YOU ARE NOT A NUMBER*

Before I introduce *The Drawing* to you, it's instructive to understand two perspectives for viewing systems like the Enneagram: 1) Bounded Set or 2) Centered Set.

Paul Hiebert, a missiologist at Fuller Seminary, put forward the idea that these two mathematical constructs could be applied to how churches operate. This was further explored in *The Shaping of Things to Come* by Michael Frost and Alan Hirsch.[1] Though I'm not talking about churches here, these two sets are worth considering in how we view and utilize personality profiles. A Bounded Set is defined by boundaries and clear definitions of what or who belongs within a certain category, and is fairly static. A Centered Set is defined by the center and the relationship of all members in the set to this center. The distance from the center, the movement toward the center, and the timing of these movements are different for each member, thus creating a dynamic, rather undefined, and ever-changing image.

So how does this apply to the Enneagram or any other system that categorizes human traits and talents into specific groups?

Bounded Set thinking comes naturally to us; our human tendency is to establish classifications and put things in them, so we can sort through all the data coming into our awareness, arrange it in some kind of order, and make sense of it all. This includes people. The categorization of nine types on the Enneagram helps us do this, giving us a "place to land," so we can understand and differentiate ourselves among the multitude of temperaments and personalities in the world. It also gives us categories for understanding other people. These are the great gifts of the Enneagram, but there are limitations to viewing people through a Bounded Set lens.

I've observed a prevailing trend to reduce the Enneagram personality types to specific and defined ways that everyone in each "type set" feels, acts, and thinks. For instance,

Bounded Set thinking says that *all* Type Fives are "this way" and that *only* people who are "this way" are Type Fives. Recently, someone told me he had done something that was apparently uncharacteristic of his particular Enneagram pattern, and someone said to him, "You can't do that; you're a Seven!" This is a misuse of the system and indicative of a Bounded Set view that has resulted in bullet points and stereotypical traits and actions for each type. It's common practice to assign one assumption, one virtue, one passion or vice, one core desire, fear, and false belief to each one of the types. Additionally, speculation about what each type longs to hear and the prominent childhood wound each type experienced puts them in a Bounded Set box.

Oh, if only we were that simple! Although these specific things are generally similar for each person who identifies with a particular Enneagram pattern, our human existence is complex, and we have a wide variety of experiences and beliefs that may not fit into our Enneagram "set." I acknowledge my own contribution to Bounded Set thinking by creating a one-page list for each type in *Self to Lose, Self to Find* and summary phrases on my presentation slides. These are meant to be reference points or guidelines, not narrow definitions of who we are and why we think, feel, and act as we do. Like an iceberg, there is so much more below the surface of our existence than what can be expressed in a few words or by the standard markers of the Enneagram types.

I became aware of the limitations and errancy of assigning each type with certain separate features when I learned that the eight passions developed by Evagrius Ponticus in AD 375—which eventually became part of the Enneagram model—were actually descriptions of troubling temptations and diversions for *everyone,* not characteristics of individual personalities. Evagrius was among the Early Church Fathers and Mothers who focused on increasing intimacy with God by mastering prayer and simple living. He listed, after careful observation, bothersome thought patterns that lured people away from their intention to pray, and were clearly problems for *everyone*: gluttony, lust, greed, sadness, acedia (akin to lack of care, or apathy), anger, vainglory, and pride. According to Evagrius, these annoying thoughts were not only disruptive to one's spiritual life, but were actually demonic temptations one needed to fight against. John Mark Comer, in his book *Live No Lies,* relates that "for Evagrius these weren't just thoughts; they were thoughts with a malignant will behind them, a dark, animating force of evil. . . . For Evagrius . . . our thought patterns are the primary demonic attack upon our souls."[2] Whoa! This puts a more serious import on the passions or vices added to the Enneagram, and how we view them.

You may be wondering how we ended up with nine vices from the original eight "disturbances." They were first revised into the "seven deadly sins" by Pope Gregory I in AD 590. He combined a few, changed acedia to sloth, and added envy to the list. Many centuries later these passions and sins were placed on the Enneagram. In a way, they were "forced to fit" the Enneagram system, with fear and deceit added to bring the total to nine.

The point is, we're all tempted and enticed by *all* the passions or vices of the types; they all block us from a full and free life with God and others. As 1 Corinthians 10:13 states, "No temptation has overtaken you except what is common to mankind." Bounded Set thinking limits pride to the Twos, gluttony to the Sevens, envy to the Fours, and so forth. I don't know about you, but I'm tempted by the passions and sins of all nine types at different times. If I only pay attention to sloth as my problem, then I miss addressing how the troubles of the other temptations affect my daily life. That said, it's also true that each type pattern generally has a "besetting sin that easily entangles" (see Hebrews 12:1)—a dominant temptation that influences thoughts, feelings, and behaviors more often and more strongly than the others.

The reality is that we all share similar fears, like feeling unworthy, unloved, and unnoticed. We all avoid many of the same things, like suffering, conflict, and failure. We all desire common things, like significance, certainty, and knowledge. We all carry false narratives and beliefs, like not measuring up or being too much or too little. What we long to hear, like "your presence matters" or "you are seen," are universal desires, and we all want and need to know much more than one or two statements to validate our purpose, our presence, and our place in the world. And, most significantly, *we are all imprinted with attributes of God,* like Divine Goodness, Love, Hope, Depth, Wisdom, Faithfulness, Joy, Power, and Peace. Some of these are our individual specialties, but we are created to express all of them.

When it comes to childhood wounds, the endless variety

and magnitude of what each person has experienced, perceived, and interpreted can't be described in a few speculative sentences, and I feel it's inappropriate and presumptive to do so. We can't assume that all people in the "set" of a type have similar childhood stories; it's just not true or possible. We are each individual "chairs" and our histories are unlike anyone else's. Each person holds personal memories and specific false narratives that need to be healed and reframed by the God who knows them and loves them fully. Inner soul restoration and transformation cannot be scripted per one's Enneagram type. Nor can it be accomplished by naming general wounds and false beliefs assumed to be exclusive to one Enneagram "set."

The use of the arrows on the Enneagram is a specific way I observe the limitations of a Bounded Set approach. I value the traditional arrows; they are very informative and helpful. They illuminate states of stress and security, identify paths of integration and disintegration, and indicate a resourceful flow of energy on the harmony triads. I'm not suggesting they're wrong or should be eliminated. But they never land anywhere; they just keep moving from number to number. In Bounded Set thinking, your options for growth and transformation are limited to the "arrow path" associated with your number, thus seeming to reduce or discourage access to the resourcefulness of all the types. As you will see, I've added other arrows to the new paradigm, which I'll explain soon; they are significant in the work of inner soul restoration and living a more centered life with God.

Bounded Set thinking also stymies curiosity about people's stories and limits our efforts to really know one another. The question "So, what's your Enneagram number?" can imply that identifying this will explain everything there is to know about you because you now fit into a known category. But the truth is that your identity and my identity can't be summed up by proclaiming our Enneagram types. There is so much more to discover about who we are, what we care about, and how we're doing. Limiting this discovery limits the degree to which we truly know others and are known by them.

Lastly, Bounded Set thinking results in a plethora of one-liners and memes filling social media posts and conversations—like suggestions for what each type wants for Christmas, or what they feel about the latest world catastrophe, or what you should say to make them happy. These may be entertaining and occasionally helpful, but they aren't always accurate and can cause confusion. More often than not, what is said about Nines (my type) rarely hits the mark of my own experience, and I am annoyed at the misrepresentation of what is actually true for me. These kinds of stereotypical, Bounded Set statements also bring up questions for people, like "What type am I really? Maybe I'm not the type I always thought I was, because what was said about another type fits me better." I hear people say more and more that they're "confused" about their type, and I surmise that this is, in part, because there's so much information to sort through and personalize, and not all of it is consistent.

I trust you see my point here about the confines of viewing the Enneagram from a Bounded Set paradigm, and why

I believe it can limit our growth toward freedom and full-ness. Although the characterization of each Enneagram type *is* a combination of common and shared patterns and traits, not everyone in each category thinks, acts, and feels the same and can be defined by the "rules" of that pattern, particularly when they expand, grow, and experience restoration and are living more fully as their Authentic Self. And we shouldn't try to force-fit everything about ourselves into our Enneagram structure. Sometimes what we think, do, and feel has nothing to do with our type, and can't be explained or understood within its narrow framework. As I explained in Chapter 4 about the stages of the Enneagram journey, categorical delineations of the types begin to lessen and will no longer typify or describe one's experience when a person responds more consistently to God's invitation to *come further in.*

This leads me to an explanation of a Centered Set perspective and a detailed description of *The Drawing.* Used with the Enneagram, I believe this perspective and the new paradigm will broaden and deepen our pilgrimage of transformation toward a more centered life with God.

CHAPTER 6

The Drawing Explained

And I, when I am lifted up from the earth, will draw all people to myself.

—JESUS, IN JOHN 12:32

There is but one good; that is God. Everything else is good when it looks to Him and bad when it turns from Him.

—C. S. LEWIS, *THE GREAT DIVORCE*

And now to *The Drawing*! I'm eager to finally share it with you! As I said earlier, this name has a double meaning: it's an actual drawing, but, of more significance, it depicts the holy attraction (the drawing) of our spirits toward God's Spirit as the ultimate destiny of our lives. It illustrates the sacred path of inner soul restoration from Adapted Self existence to Authentic Self living. I believe it is a much-needed adjunct to the classic Enneagram system.

As you'll see, *The Drawing* is a simple structure of concentric circles formed around an inner triangle with arrows pointing toward the middle, making it a Centered Set model because all members in the set are related to the central point. The center in this new image, the triangle, is representative of the triune God: God the Creator, God the Christ, and God the indwelling Holy Spirit—and the space surrounding it is our Spiritual Center, where we enjoy a relational union with the Divine. More on that in a minute. At this point, you may be wondering, "Who are the *members* of this Centered Set then?" The answer is: *Everyone!* I believe *all* people are related to God and have a Spiritual Center. *All* people are being drawn by God toward the center, whether they realize it or not. "From the center of the soul," Saint Teresa of Ávila teaches, "God is calling. The driving force of our existence is our longing to find our way home to him."[1]

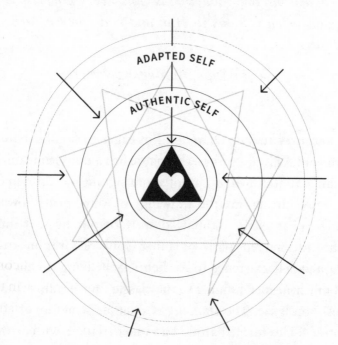

I'll explain the meaning of each element in several steps, starting in the middle and building outward, much like a camera zooming in to highlight details and then out to get a broader view. Once all of the elements are described, the basic version as seen above will make sense, and can be easily accessed and utilized without including all of the words on the following figures.

The triangle in the middle of *The Drawing* is a common symbol for the Triune God. In the middle of this triangle is the shape of a heart, representing Love, for Love comes from God and God is Love (1 John 4:7–8). God's unending, unconditional, and inseparable love is paramount and is the core of our very existence. Romans 8:38–39 assures us "that nothing can ever separate us from God's love. Neither death nor life, neither angels nor demons, neither our fears for today nor our worries about tomorrow—not even the powers of hell can separate us from God's love. No power in the sky above or in the earth below—indeed, nothing in all creation will ever be able to separate us from the love of God that is revealed in Christ Jesus our Lord" (NLT).

Richard Rohr, in his book *The Divine Dance: The Trinity and Your Transformation,* offers two visual images for the Triune God; one is a divine dance and the other is a shared table. "Whatever is going on in God is a *flow,* a *radical relatedness,* a perfect *communion* between Three—a circle dance of love. And God is not just a dancer, God is the dance itself." Rohr also shares about an iconic art piece called *The Trinity* created by Andrei Rublev in the fifteenth century. Rohr describes the piece as an illustration of "The Holy One in the form of Three—eating and

drinking, in infinite hospitality and utter enjoyment be-
tween themselves. If we take the depiction of God in *The
Trinity* seriously, we have to say, 'In the beginning was the
Relationship.' "

On Rublev's painting there appears to be a rectangular
space on the front; some surmise that a mirror was glued
to the table there. According to Rohr, this would imply that
the observer of the art is also invited to be a participant
in the fellowship of the Trinity around the table. Rohr encourages his readers "to take this image into yourself . . . to
recognize that this Table is not reserved exclusively for the
Three, nor is the divine circle dance a closed circle; we're all
invited in. All creation is invited in, and this is the libera-
tion God intended from the very beginning."[2]

So, in other words, when we are invited by God to *come
further in,* we are being drawn into a relationship, to a fellowship, to a divine dance with God the Creator, God the
Christ, and God the Spirit. This is depicted by the center
triangle and heart on *The Drawing.*

Divine attributes that initiate and flow from the Source

of Love radiate out from this center, and are represented by words on the surrounding circle. An unlimited number of words could be included here as characteristics of God, but I've chosen the "fruit of the Spirit" as found in Galatians 5:22–23, and additional words representing the divine gifts of the Enneagram types as I noted in *Self to Lose, Self to Find*.

The inspiration for this element of *The Drawing* came from two insightful books. The first is a compilation of addresses by Evelyn Underhill, an English scholar, speaker, and writer I greatly admire for her practical explanation of Christian spirituality and mysticism. *The Fruits of the Spirit* was published in 1942, a year after her death. What intrigued me most about her presentation of these virtues was that "love" is not packaged with the other eight, but is the central starting point from which all the other qualities grow, like flower petals spreading out from the central bud.

The Fruits of the Spirit are those dispositions, those ways of thinking, speaking and acting, which are brought forth in us, gradually but inevitably, by the pressure of Divine Love in our souls. They all spring from that one root.[3]

Love therefore is the budding point from which all the rest come: that tender, cherishing attitude; that unlimited self-forgetfulness, generosity and kindness which is the attitude of God to all His creatures and so must be the attitude towards them which His Spirit brings forth in us. If that is frostbitten, we need not hope for any of the rest.[4]

Pastor Randy Rowland offers a similar perspective in his book *The Sins We Love: Embracing Brokenness, Hoping for Wholeness*:

The fruit of the Spirit is love. . . . Sin is a distortion of perfect love. The fruit of the Spirit works against the power of decay by imprinting the perfect love of God on our very essence. That same perfect love takes root in our essence and grows outward, transforming us, Paul says, "from one state of glory to another into the image of Christ." . . . Love sprouts joy, peace, patience, gentleness, self-control, and all the other fruit.[5]

The truth is this: your life will be characterized by the fruit of the Spirit and by divine qualities as you cultivate your Spiritual Center and respond to God's ongoing invitation to *come further in*. As I shared in *Self to Lose, Self to Find,* if we are in the middle of the circle, we are equidistant from all the Enneagram types. This means that the more our lives are centered with God, the more we will experience and express all the divine attributes and the "wow" qualities of all the types. You will naturally embody more joy, more peace, more patience, more kindness, more goodness, more faithfulness, more gentleness, more self-control, more hope, more depth, more wisdom, and more power. I certainly want these qualities to characterize my life, and I assume you do as well.

The next circle is the expanded space around the center, representing your Authentic Self. This is your true "home," where your needs are met, your desires fulfilled, and you live most fully and freely as your true, God-gifted self. In this space, the "affirming love voice" of the Spirit tells your own spirit the truth of who you really are: *you are worthy, you are beloved, you are valued, you are whole, you are known, you are accepted, you are enough, you are protected, you are significant,* and so many other realities. This is where you can hear the "sound of the genuine" in you, as named by Howard Thurman in a sermon at Spelman College. "There is something that waits and listens for the sound of the genuine in yourself. Nobody like you has ever been born and no one like you will ever be born again—you are the only one. And if you miss the sound of the genuine in you, you will be a cripple all the rest of your life, because you will never be able to get a scent on who you are."[6]

It is also from the inner space that your true Authentic Self, designed to reflect the image of God in a unique and holy way, shines forth, radiating light and love outward to the world.

> *Always visualize your soul as vast, spacious, and plentiful. . . . The soul's capacity far transcends our imagining. The sun at the center of this place radiates to every part.*
>
> —SAINT TERESA OF ÁVILA, *THE INTERIOR CASTLE*[7]

The next two additions are the circles that represent your Adapted Self. The outermost circle is like a brick wall built with self-protective strategies, fears, avoidances, defenses, false beliefs, wounds, compulsions, deceptions, perceptions, sins, and other habitual patterns that are internal strongholds and barriers inhibiting freedom of movement toward the center.

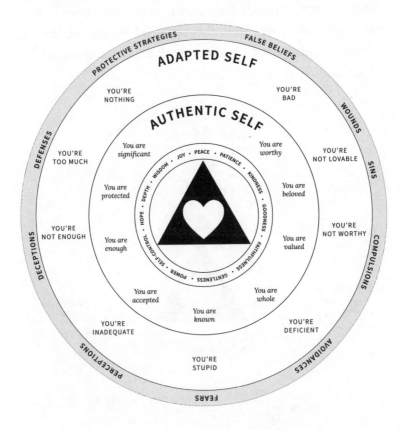

Adjacent to this outer circle is where you frequently hear the "accusing fear voice," taunting you, paralyzing you, and condemning you with false accusations: *you're bad, you're not lovable, you're not worthy, you're deficient, you're stupid, you're inadequate, you're not enough, you're too much, you're nothing,* and on and on. We all can easily fill in this space with other condemnations that consistently plague us.

A primal step in the work of inner soul restoration is to name the specific false narratives and strongholds that consistently cycle through your heart, mind, and body. These two outer circles represent this essential awareness, leading to inner healing and a clearer pathway to a centered life with God.

The next key addition is a number of arrows, all pointing toward the middle. These represent our pilgrimages toward home, toward our union with God, toward the full actualization of our God-created Authentic Selves. Most significantly, they demonstrate that the Holy One in the center is drawing us to where *true integration, true restoration* takes place. In reality, this picture should include millions of arrows, each one symbolizing every single person, *all* the members in this Centered Set. Note the arrows are of different lengths, since everyone is on their own spiritual

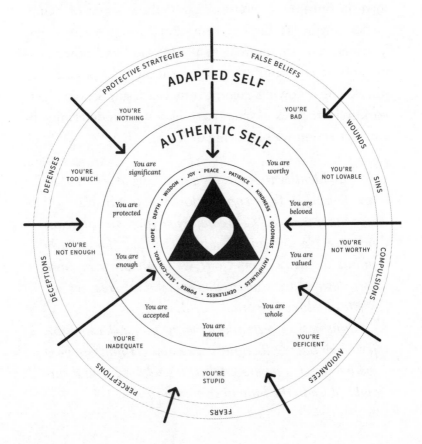

journey. And, of course, our pilgrimages are never straight paths like the arrows, but more like the twists and turns of a labyrinth. Yet, these arrows indicate the direction in which we're invited to turn and travel on our lifetime pilgrimage to the center. Even though all the arrows point inward, this doesn't mean that everyone is facing the middle or willingly traveling along a path toward it.

To capture what I'm suggesting for the arrows in *The Drawing,* a brief understanding of "consolation" and "desolation" is clarifying. Saint Ignatius of Loyola, who developed the Spiritual Exercises, classified our states of being, particularly our feelings and emotions, into two categories: "consolation," the movement toward God and other people, and "desolation," the movement away from God and others. The following excerpt from the Jesuit Schools Network website gives us clues as to how we can determine in which direction we're moving or facing:

> *We can identity these states by looking at where they are pointing. True consolation points toward God and other people. We are happy, joyous, and at peace because we are joined with others. . . . Desolation points us away from God. We're unhappy because our desires are thwarted. People don't respect us. We're all alone in a cruel world.*
>
> *Consolation feels like coming home. Desolation feels like having lost our way home. Home is where we belong. It's where God is. It's where we find our right place in the human community.*[8]

When I participated in a yearlong experience of the Spiritual Exercises of Saint Ignatius, my spiritual director gave me two pictures as a guide to determine whether I was in a state of consolation or desolation. The image for consolation is a smooth oval shape with a variety of words inside including *gratitude, courage, patience, flexibility, grace of tears,* and *vulnerability.* The caption at the bottom describing the state of consolation reads: *The realization in faith that God loves me and is very near, and a movement or drawing toward God.* The image for desolation is a jagged oval with a similar variety of words, like *impatience, compulsion, self-rejection, perfectionism, disorder, exaggeration,* and *avoidance of prayer.* The caption for desolation reads: *Belief that God is absent, not loving me. A sense of separation from God, a drawing away from God.*

States of consolation and desolation are not static; they fluctuate depending on our reactions and responses during the ins and outs of our daily lives. They are good indicators of the direction we're facing—toward God and the freedom of our Authentic Selves, or away from God and toward the trappings of our Adapted Self beliefs and strategies.

The arrows pointing from the outside toward the middle raise some fundamental questions for our spiritual awareness: Where is your attention focused in relation to the middle: Are you moving away from it or toward it? Are you moving along the path of consolation or of desolation, of integration or of disintegration? As Jeff Imbach asked in *The River Within: Loving God, Living Passionately*, "The question is not, 'Where is God?' The question is rather, 'Where are we?'"⁹

Let's unpack this a little more. In most descriptions of the Enneagram types, a common element is the "focus of attention" for each one. This is important to identify because where we place our attention largely determines where our energy is directed, and this, in turn, will influence our thoughts, feelings and behaviors. Naming what we focus on gives us the option to shift our attention away from one thing to something else if we choose. Considering the nine Enneagram types and a general focus of attention for each, here are possible shifts we all can adopt:

- From what's wrong to what's right
- From the demanding needs of others to self-care
- From individual goals to collaboration with others
- From what's missing to what's here
- From what makes sense to embracing mystery
- From what could go wrong to peace about whatever happens
- From what's next to what's present
- From being tough to being vulnerable
- From the expectations of others to personal priorities

In a broader sense, then, where your attention is focused and in which direction you are turned—whether away from God, where you are stuck in Adapted Self patterns, or toward the center with God, where your Authentic Self flourishes—will determine the trajectory of your energy and whether it keeps you stagnant and constricted or enables you to grow and flourish. The focus of your attention will influence what you release and what you cling to, whether you feel good about yourself or not, whether you cultivate more divine qualities, and, in general, your sense of well-being and fulfillment. Simply acknowledging where our attention and energy are directed helps us know "where we are."

Now, you may be wondering, "Where does the Enneagram fit on *The Drawing*?" I've placed it between the inner sanctum and the outer void. It serves as a portal, an opening to greater self-awareness and a doorway for greater ac-

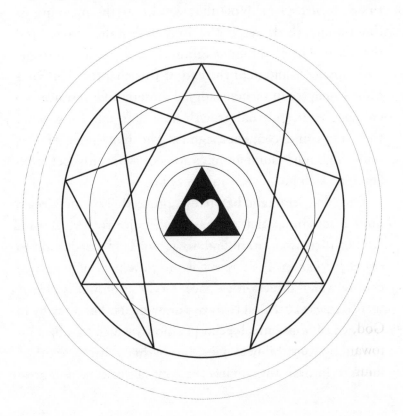

cess to the inner reality of your Spiritual Center and your connection with God. The Enneagram tool helps identify the barriers of your Adapted Self that impede movement toward the center, and provides an understanding of the wounds to be healed, the repeating habits to alter, and the false narratives to be reframed. The Enneagram is a gift on the pilgrimage to the center, but it has limited value by itself.

And there you have it—*The Drawing*! Simple yet profound. I believe it offers a broader and deeper comprehension of the sacred spiritual pilgrimage and God's invitation to *come further in*. Now that you know the meaning of the triangle, the heart, the various circles, the arrows, and the placement of the Enneagram, I refer you again to the basic image found near the end of this chapter. This simplified image can more easily be understood and used to enhance your spiritual growth now that you know what the circles and elements signify. The remainder of this book highlights some implications of what this Centered Set approach means for our everyday lives.

One final thought before we proceed. I've mentioned quite a few times that we have the choice to turn toward God or turn away from God; to accept God's invitation to *come further in* or to reject it. Yet, even though we can choose which direction we face, God's attention is always turned toward us! God is always drawing us. This may fly in the face of some theological positions, which can be supported by some biblical texts, but perhaps there's another, more scriptural way to view the continuous gaze and presence of God. Brad Jersak, author of several books including *A More Christlike God: A More Beautiful Gospel*, created a powerful dramatization of this truth called "The Gospel in Chairs," available for viewing online. I encourage you to check it out.[10]

Essentially, God's primary disposition toward us is not wrath and enmity; God does not turn away from us or abandon us, although it may feel like it sometimes, especially when we hit the Wall or go through dark, lonely, and troubling seasons in our lives. God's primary disposition toward us is Love, and God will keep orienting toward us no matter how much or how often we turn and look the other way. God has come to us, clothed in Jesus, to express Divine Love and to heal us and reclaim our Authentic Selves. God will continue to draw us to the center of Love through circumstances, whispers in our spirits, the Scriptures, other people, music, nature, and in any way God knows we might respond and be transformed by this Love. God will find a way to get our attention; we have the choice to respond or not. The God who created us sees us, loves us, and desires for each of us to live fully and freely as our Authentic Selves, and to enjoy holy fellowship with the Triune One. The invitation to *come further in* is always offered.

And, the complete truth is that God is *always with us* through the Holy Spirit, within and around us. Our dear granddaughter signs all of her communications to us with *I love you, NMW,* which stands for "no matter what." She scribbled this on her early drawings and still writes this today as a teenager. This is just how Jesus finished His final message after His resurrection, as recorded in Matthew 28:20: "And surely I am with you always, to the very end of the age." NMW!

As you ponder *The Drawing*—this fresh paradigm with the centrality of love in the middle, radiating divine qualities, and affirming love truths; with the outer barriers and accusations from the fear voice; with the regular Enneagram drawing and with the arrows all pointing toward the center—take in these words from Saint Teresa of Ávila as a summarizing statement: "The process of the spiritual life consists of an inward journey in which a person's consciousness moves from the outer, sensory realm toward God at the inmost center."[11]

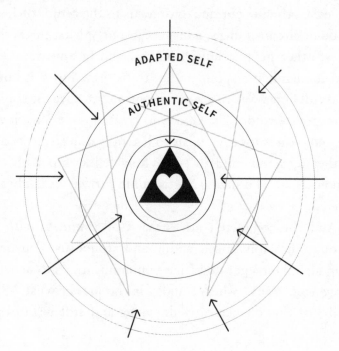

Looking ahead to Section III with *The Drawing* in mind, consider these questions: What is a more centered life with the Triune God, the divine dance, actually like? What will we know and experience more often, and how will our everyday realities change, when we move from the outer circumference of our separate, ego-driven self toward the center of our spirit in union with God's Spirit? Who will we become on our spiritual pilgrimage while our Authentic Self is being reclaimed and restored, and as we *come further in*? To address these essential questions, we'll explore together seven movements *from* one state of being *to* another:

From What I Am *to* Who I Am
From Reactive *to* Responsive
From Bondage *to* Freedom
From Wounded *to* Whole
From Shakable *to* Unshakable
From Burdened *to* Rested
From Glory *to* Glory

These movements are inspired by key biblical texts, and are enhanced by stories from my own life and the lives of others. I trust you will find these movements to be inspiring, hopeful, and liberating!

SECTION III

Movements Toward the Center

There is a road
that runs straight through your heart
Walk on it.
To be a pilgrim means
to be on the move, slowly
to notice your luggage becoming lighter
to be seeking for treasures that do not rust
to be comfortable with your heart's questions
to be moving toward the holy ground of home
with empty hands and bare feet.
And yet, you cannot reach that home
until you've loved the pilgrim in you
One must be comfortable
with pilgrimhood
before one's feet can touch the homeland.
Do you want to go home?
There's a road that runs
straight through your heart.
Walk on it.

—MACRINA WIEDERKEHR, "TOURIST OR PILGRIM?," FROM
SEASONS OF YOUR HEART: PRAYERS AND REFLECTIONS

CHAPTER 7

From What I Am
to Who I Am

Jesus came to announce to us that an identity based on success, popularity, and power is a false identity—an illusion! Loudly and clearly he says: "You are not what the world makes you; but you are children of God."

—HENRI J. M. NOUWEN, *HERE AND NOW*

You are created to experience true life, your genuine identity, your deepest meaning, your fullest purpose, and your ultimate value in an intimate, loving union with God at the core of your being.

—M. ROBERT MULHOLLAND JR., *THE DEEPER JOURNEY*

What we believe about our identity and how we view ourselves impact every aspect of our lives. Along the path of pilgrimage to a more centered life with the Triune God, the movement of our identity awareness *from* What I Am *to*

Who I Am—*from* Adapted Self labels *to* Authentic Self being—is a vital part of our spiritual growth and flourishing. As we are drawn toward God, we will experience the vital shift *from* defining ourselves with limiting constructs *to* describing ourselves as persons created to be in union with God and ones who freely reflect God's image in unique and holy ways.

The apostle Paul recognized the insignificance of labels and categories in contrast to our larger identity of belonging to Christ. "There is neither Jew nor Gentile, neither slave nor free, nor is there male and female, for *you are all one in Christ Jesus*" (Galatians 3:28, emphasis mine). This reminds us that our identity is not our ethnicity, our position, our gender, our religion, or any other category with which we're tempted to label ourselves and others. We are God's people—one in Christ—all of us.

What identity markers are like sticky notes defining What You Are? These could be from what others have told you, like "you're dumb" or "you're too emotional"; from what you do, like "I'm an accountant" or "I'm an athlete"; from how you appear, like "I have to look good" or "I'm fat"; from how you feel about yourself, like "I'm a failure" or "I'm incompetent"; and from groups you associate with, like "I'm a Presbyterian" or "I'm a liberal" or "I'm an Enneagram Four." Pause for a moment and consider some of the nametags you consistently wear to characterize yourself.

Labels can be negative or positive. Generally, the unfavorable ones create false and wounding narratives that we hold about ourselves. When we assume these are true, we remain stuck in repeating patterns of thinking, feeling, and behaving that reflect these beliefs, like being trapped in the outer circles of *The Drawing*. Positive labels help affirm our giftedness, our outstanding qualities, and our unique contributions. We need these to remind us of our true essence. But they can also become ego attachments we hide behind or rely on to define our identity. For instance, there is a difference between trying to maintain a "good girl" or "good boy" status to feel worthy of admiration in the eyes of others, and knowing deep in your core that you're a good and worthwhile person.

Many stories are woven throughout the Scriptures of people who were given new names, new identities. A few powerful examples are Abram becoming Abraham, Sarai becoming Sarah, Jacob becoming Israel, Simon becoming Peter, and Saul becoming Paul. They all moved from one way of understanding themselves to a greater awareness of how God viewed them and the nature of their divine destinies. I have personally experienced life-changing shifts when my heart and mind were opened to prayerfully seeing myself, not through my own eyes or the eyes of others, but through God's eyes. And I've witnessed similar shifts in those I meet with when together we've invited God to reveal something about their truest, most authentic selves. Though the topic of identity can be complex, true life stories are simple and real. As we consider the movement *from* What I Am *to* Who I Am, I offer three such stories from Talia, Margaret, and Marcus. Included in their stories are two identity exercises I've learned and often utilize to guide the process of experiencing this crucial, life-changing shift.

Talia came to me for spiritual direction because she was longing for a more vibrant and consistent life with God. Recurring themes for Talia over the course of our time together were discouragement, self-doubt, and a lack of direction. She often spoke about herself unfavorably: "I know I should . . . I'm forgetful . . . I'm just so inconsistent," along with other disparaging personal labels. This was especially true when she talked about her struggle to set aside time for her own personal reflections with God. During one particular session with me, she mentioned her self-judgment and lack of contentment with who she was and how she lived. "I so often doubt and question myself, and I'm not sure why I get those feelings, but they get me down."

I invited her to engage in an identity exercise, which she was willing to do. I learned this particular exercise from my friend and life coach Shannon Bruce. I've used variations of it with countless individuals and in groups, most often with transformational outcomes. The process starts with writing a list of ten adjectives that describe you when you're at your best and feel good about yourself. These are not activities, but high-quality attributes. People often say how hard this is, and that it's much easier to name their negative characteristics. Once this list is compiled, you add qualities that others who know you well would say about you. The next step is the Holy Aha part! While reading through the list, you visualize standing back and observing an imaginary person who embodies the qualities you've written, someone you would look at objectively, not subjectively like you do when looking at yourself. While considering this person, you pause to ask God to reveal a name for her or him that captures these qualities, using both an adjective and an object. Is there an image that comes to mind? Do one or two words pop up? I tell people to allow whatever comes into their awareness as the Holy Spirit guides them, and not to censor or dismiss it. Examples of a name might be Deep Ocean or Regal Lion.

Talia's affirmative list included *confident, loving, loyal, joyful, peaceful, content, thoughtful, compassionate, prayerful, dedicated,* and *hopeful.* As she sat in silence considering these qualities and prayerfully considering a name, she lifted her head and said with a big smile, "Bright Sun! I see a sun and it's bright. Yes, that is me at my best!" As we unpacked this a bit, she told me that she loves images of the sun and uses them often in her home and garden decor. They bring her joy and speak to her of life and light. Then she told me she had just purchased a picture at an art exhibition, titled *And the Sun Came Out.* As she connected the significance of her newly revealed name and the coincidence of her new purchase, she said, "Well, isn't that a fitting message for me?"

The next time we met, Talia said she was really owning her new name, Bright Sun. "It feels like a new responsibility, like it's my purpose to be this. I want to be warm and welcoming. It really is who I am and how I like to be. Realizing this brings me a new lightness." This identity awareness moved Talia *from* the false narrative of What She Is—as doubtful, lazy, inconsistent, and incapable—*to* the truth of Who She Is as Bright Sun. Knowing this true identity now informs her life, her activities, and her relationships. The revelation didn't put a complete stop to Talia's struggle with self-doubt and direction, but when she finds herself dragged down by discouragement, she reminds herself that her authentic identity is Bright Sun. This dispels her self-critical thoughts and gives her renewed energy and confidence.

Next is Margaret's story. Margaret and I had been meeting for a few months when she shared that she felt like something new was being birthed in her. She was desiring to base her identity more on what God thinks of her, but admitted she wasn't there yet. She was starting to realize that her security and self-esteem were dependent on success in her work, on other people's impressions of her and her family, and on her ability to take care of everything on her own because of her strength and independence—indications she was basing her identity on What She Was. In spite of appearing tough and confident, inside she was unsure of herself.

At this point in our conversation, I asked Margaret if she would like to go through an identity exercise, to which she agreed. I learned this process from my friends Jamie and Donna Winship of Identity Exchange. A more extensive explanation of the exercise is included in their online course called Becoming What You Believe, which you can find on their website. I encourage you to check it out![1] They graciously gave me permission to offer a mini-version of it here. Like the other exercise, this one includes making a list, but with this activity you ask God to reveal the negative labels you've come to believe about yourself based on past experiences, what others have said about you, and your own perceptions. Margaret's list included *you're not enough, you're all alone, you're not pretty enough, you are judged, you don't measure up, you don't fit any place perfectly,* and *you have to take care of yourself.* After making the initial list, the next step is to imagine that Jesus comes to you and you give Him the list. The next two questions are critical: What does Jesus do with the list? and What do you notice about Him? In Margaret's case, she saw Jesus rip it up. She sensed great love, kindness, and understanding toward her in His eyes. (During all the times I've directed this exercise, no one has said that Jesus looks at the list with judgment or condemnation; He always dismisses it in some way.)

The final part of this exercise is to ask Jesus to show you something about your true identity, and to reveal how He sees you and what He calls you. This could be a word, an image, or an impression. Again, I tell people to simply receive whatever comes into their mind; it may not make any sense initially. After we quietly and prayerfully waited together, Margaret said that what she saw was the snow-covered trees she had passed by recently; the sun had been shining on them and they were sparkling like brilliant diamonds. The name that came to her was Sparkling Joy. Her response was, "I like it! I realize I need to let go of trying to be something or someone else, and just be this. It's really a picture of who I am. I do want to be more joyful and more sparkly." Margaret shifted *from* relying on the way others saw her *to* how God saw her.

The third and final story is about Marcus, and it includes elements of both exercises. Marcus contacted me to learn more about his Enneagram type and how it was affecting his relationships. Over the course of a few months, he related a difficult relational experience that had rocked his sense of confidence. Because of it, he noticed he was retreating from other interactions. He felt stuck as he tried to figure out why the relational break had happened. He was tense and uptight, and was riddled with self-criticism. He felt stupid and embarrassed. He mentioned that he was feeling cold and closed-off from himself and God, and admitted that when he's more open and receptive to God, he is more solid, secure, grounded, and engaging.

Marcus was reminded of an image he'd received when he attended a conference presented by the Winships. He had gone through the steps of making a list and handing it to Jesus, but when it came to receiving his true identity, all he saw was a plank of wood. At the time, it didn't mean much to him and it felt rather insignificant, confusing, and boring. Yet, as he began to unpack it more in our conversation, he realized that this image really resonated with his best attributes. He related that a solid piece of wood has a deep reverberating sound when you knock on it. It is uniform but, if you look closer, it has unique intricacies, and it is sturdy and durable. Marcus also visualized this piece of wood in God's hand as something useful and active, rather than plain and passive. "This is who I really am at my best and who I like to be." This awareness shifted Marcus *from* being insecure and critical *to* being grounded and assured.

As a follow-up to this initial conversation with Marcus, he wrote the following update when I contacted him for permission to use his story:

*I remember you suggested to look for a wooden ob-
ject or symbol that represented this moment. I
couldn't find anything for a while so I settled on a
wood-inspired desktop background for the last few
years. But I finally saved up enough money to buy a
Live Edge wooden bench. It's next to the chair where
I sit to do my morning prayer and reading. It's a great
reminder for my soul. I often reach over and knock on
it with my knuckles, just to hear the solid sound.*

In all three stories, the negative and discouraging beliefs
Talia, Margaret, and Marcus held about themselves were
changed when they were awakened to a "new name" that
reflected their true, God-breathed identity. They switched
from hearing the accusing fear voice to hearing the affirming love voice. This can be your story too.

The starting point for knowing Who You Are is to first
believe that you were created by God and that you have
been known and loved by God from the very beginning of
your existence. The Psalmist penned, "I praise you for I am
fearfully and wonderfully made," and "Your eyes saw my
unformed body" (Psalm 139:14, 16). If we can confidently
rest in this truth, we won't be assailed by the lies that tell us
otherwise, like the fear voice accusations of our Adapted
Self patterns.

Another important realization for Who You Are is
knowing that you, yes *you,* were created for a holy purpose.
Near the beginning of Jesus's discourse in the Sermon on
the Mount, He looked at a ragtag group of followers and

proclaimed words of identity, calling them to be an influence in the world: "You are the salt of the earth" and "You are the light of the world" (Matthew 5:13, 14). There was nothing spectacular about these people; they were simple, ordinary men and women curious about a man named Jesus who was teaching and healing throughout the countryside. Some of them became His closest friends and disciples. Jesus considers you the same way—one He dearly loves who has an extraordinary identity and glorious destiny!

I could list many scriptures that remind us of Who We Are, like Ephesians 2:10: "For we are God's handiwork, created in Christ Jesus to do good works, which God prepared in advance for us to do." Other scriptures tell us we are valued, beloved, and seen, and that we belong in God's family as children and heirs. I think the most powerful and profound reality of our holy identity is that we are containers for the Holy Spirit, that we are indwelled by the Spirit of the Living God. "Do you not know that your bodies are temples of the Holy Spirit, who is in you, whom you have received from God?" (1 Corinthians 6:19). That is an astounding truth—to be filled with the Holy Spirit of God is a miraculous mystery and a key identifier of Who You Are!

Hearing from God about your individual identity will move you from a narrow definition of What I Am to a liberating realization of Who I Am. I had a lived experience of this truth when I returned home from a week of speaking in the Dominican Republic. Back home, I had no idea if my presence and my presentation would have any lasting impact, and I couldn't help but wonder what the people I had spoken to thought of me and my message. I was focusing on "what" I was, and whether that "what" had been enough. I then asked God about my identity and if there was anything about this situation God wanted me to know. I paused, listened, and heard in my spirit, *"You are my messenger."* Then a picture of a messenger in stories like *Downton Abbey* came into my mind. They pick up an envelope from one house, ride their bike to another house, and deliver the envelope to the desired recipient. The messenger has no idea what's in the envelope, only that it's meant to be delivered. The messenger then rides away, having completed the assigned task, without any knowledge as to the meaning or outcome of the enclosed message. As I pondered this picture in light of hearing that I was God's messenger, I realized that if I'm entrusted with delivering a message God gives me, then that's all I'm obligated to do. What the message means to any recipient is not for me to always know, and any outcomes from the message are God's concern, not mine. This awareness set me free in that moment from worrying about my work in the Dominican Republic, and it has also set me free in the work I'm privileged to do. I consider it a holy honor and high calling to be God's messenger!

What about you? Are you locked into an identity determined by the sticky notes of What You Are—on what you do, what you think about yourself, what groups define you, and what you've been told? Pause again and reflect on the definitions and labels that keep you stuck and distracted on the outer edges of your Adapted Self. Turn your attention toward God and release them, knowing the list you hold is not valid and that God ignores it. Receive the truth that you

are a beloved child of God, created with a true God-given
identity and a holy purpose, and you are a sacred vessel for
the Holy Spirit. Ask God to show you your specific true
identity; listen and embrace what you hear. Claim this with
clarity on Who You Are, and allow the Spirit to reveal more
and more of what this means in your everyday life.

I also encourage you to find others who will support you
on this pilgrimage toward living as your Authentic Self,
those who will reinforce your true identity. For example,
about eight years ago, my dear friend Linda and I were in a
coaching group that went through the first exercise I explained to you. At the time, God gave us both specific names
we shared with one another. Since then, Linda and I call
each other Powerful Beauty and Radiant Rock when we
communicate. This simple and fun habit reminds us both
of our God-given identities, and oftentimes we need this
fresh nudge to remember Who We Are.

As God continues to invite you to *come further in* and as
you continue to respond in the posture of a pilgrim, your
truest and best self will be reclaimed and restored to its
original holy design. You will no longer be defined and held
back by false narratives and negative labels. You will move
from knowing yourself by What I Am *to* freely living as
Who I Am, steadily walking in the fullness of your true,
God-given identity!

CHAPTER 8

From Reactive *to* Responsive

Our outward behavior, particularly our reactivity and how readily it gets triggered, is the visible result of what might have happened to us early on, the evidence of what is driving us subconsciously—either holding us hostage or potentiating us beautifully.

—DAVID DANIELS, M.D., AND SUZANNE DION,
THE ENNEAGRAM, RELATIONSHIPS, AND INTIMACY

Once we become aware of the patterns that persist in our own life, it's as if the blinders have been removed. We can start to see why we act the way we do.

—MEREDITH MCDANIEL, *IN WANT + PLENTY*

On the pilgrimage to a more centered life with God, we will become less dominated by our reactions and more guided by our responses. What's the difference? In general, reactions are immediate, urgent, and without conscious thought. They are like knee-jerk impulses and are usually triggered by emotions that result in compulsive actions. Responses are thoughtful and intelligent replies, resulting from taking time to consider outcomes and determine the best course of action in a situation.

Reacting is a natural part of being human. But overreacting creates all sorts of problems in our relationships, in our physical health, in our work environments, and in just about every area of our lives. Because it happens so quickly, we often aren't even aware that we're reacting beyond what a situation requires or justifies. It's like a train picks us up and we're speeding down the track of reactivity before we even realize it. Usually when we enter into an emotionally reactive state, it's tied to a deeper narrative embedded in our subconscious, just waiting to be ignited by a perception, action, or comment by another person or circumstance. This narrative is likely attached to repeated patterns developed from childhood experiences. The past will flood the present, causing old ingrained beliefs and fears to flare up.

Teresa and I have met for spiritual direction for a few years. A repetitive theme has been the nagging voice of her inner critic. During one session, she shared with me a Holy Aha moment when she realized how reactive and overwhelmed with self-judgment she becomes when she doesn't live up to her own expectations. She related a time when she was in charge of leading a workshop. In the middle of the presentation, she was interrupted and questioned by someone on her team about the content. She froze and then muddled through to the end. When it was over, her immediate reaction was to dismiss the whole workshop as a failure and to shame herself. She wasn't able to step back and evaluate the situation rationally; she could focus only on what she viewed as her total inadequacy. Self-loathing crowded her mind, and her chest clenched into a tight wad of disappointment and embarrassment. Fear of what her coworkers thought gripped her, and she was sure they would finally realize she was incompetent and would no longer want to work with her.

Teresa shoved her feelings down, not giving any room for their expression. She admitted to me that she usually views her emotions as a sign of weakness, and definitely does not want anyone else to see them. "I've separated myself from my feelings, and always wonder what's wrong with me if I cry. I try as best I can to keep a tight rein on my emotions. I hate that I'm emotional, but sometimes I just can't help it."

I invited Teresa to think of an image that represented her feelings. She thought of waves in the ocean. "They just happen; they crest and come back down again. But, I always try to put a barrier up so I won't be swamped. I can see that if I would just ride the waves, the rise and fall of my emotions, I would be less rigid and critical of myself." Teresa sensed the possibility of responding differently in the future. She could pause and give space for her emotions, rather than reacting so quickly, criticizing herself, and shutting down her feelings.

Teresa identified that her pattern of reacting with self-criticism when she's not perfect and when she feels strong emotions stems from a painful situation in her childhood. She was very close to her grandparents; they had always been there for her and would praise her for being an outstanding student and good girl. When she was eight years old, they suddenly cut off all ties with her family. She didn't know why. In her young mind, she thought it was because she had disappointed them and therefore they didn't want a relationship with her anymore. This situation also created a lot of anguish for her parents, so Teresa buried her sadness to keep from adding more strain in their home. Years later, the rejection by her grandparents for what she believed was her fault still activates a strong reaction in her if she doesn't perform perfectly. She fears being abandoned again for her wrong behavior. Teresa also dismisses her emotions for fear of looking out of control or causing problems for others. We'll look at Teresa's story a bit more later.

Exploring our internal patterns and identifying how they trigger impulses, both inwardly and outwardly, is a vital part of our pilgrimage toward living more fully in the center of our life with God. We will move *from* being reactive *to* being more responsive.

Let's look at three aspects of patterns and patterning that will shed more light on our propensity to overreact. First of all, a pattern is a sequence that is repeated over and over. Once recognized and identified, our internal patterns can be interrupted and reframed, opening up alternative choices of response. Secondly, false belief patterns and developed ways of thinking, acting, and feeling can become strongholds of reactivity, and places where we're attacked and accused by the enemy of our souls, the force that wants to "steal, kill, and destroy" us (John 10:10). Thirdly, patterns provide templates for creating new responses, so determining the right patterns to follow for our spiritual growth toward freedom is imperative.

The Power of Repetitive Patterns

We are creatures of habit. As much as we'd like to think we operate with freedom of choice most of the time, we generally don't. Our lives are dictated and ordered by sequential patterns. Some are quite necessary, like breathing and sleeping. Most of our patterns are habitual and common, and once they've been established, we employ them without our conscious awareness. For instance, we generally start and end each day with the same routines. Patterns also help us sort and categorize all the stimuli we encounter minute-by-minute. Without the ability to form patterns from what we observe—without recognition of objects, locations, people, symbols, and information that provide us with predictability and organization—our lives would be in complete chaos. Repetitive patterns are necessary for our survival and well-being.

Yet patterns can also keep us stuck in emotional, mental, and behavioral habits that fuel our reactivity. The beliefs we developed early in life about who we need to be and how we need to act were born out of repetition, reinforcement, and systems of perceived rewards and punishments. These contributed to the formation of our Adapted Self persona. They linger in our subconscious and greatly influence how and why we react in certain situations. Habitual reactions in the past are often projected into the present time, feeling very current and real, as Teresa experienced.

Some belief patterns are helpful and life-giving, enhancing our sense of well-being. Some patterns were useful at one time, but then cease to work well for us and, ultimately, become barriers to freedom. Other beliefs are restrictive and hurtful, holding us hostage to negative and false narratives that play over and over in our subconscious minds, and trigger strong reactions like anger, shame, and fear. In order to be released from the power and pervasiveness of false and limiting beliefs, and to experience the inner soul restoration that will set us free, it is necessary to "mine memories" in the caverns of our subconscious, unearthing the sedimentary patterns that have settled in our souls.

Why mine memories? I became more aware of the value and validity of revisiting past memories in order to become more consciously responsive in the present time during a training conference on The Healing Timeline, presented by Catherine Thorpe, MA, a licensed mental health counselor. In her book by the same name, Thorpe explains the step-by-step process of how to effectively access and address former experiences that are triggering a current reaction; I won't give the details here, but I certainly recommend her work. The overall basis for the process Thorpe developed is the scientific understanding of the brain. "*Neuroplasticity* is the term scientists have given to the brain's impressive ability to change its structure and function in response to experience. . . . Brain research reveals humans can rewire their brains as needed . . . The brain's capacity for renewal and re-generation is remarkable."[1]

In other words, we can change our reactions and find new ways to respond. Yet, if you don't know what's hidden in the inner recesses of your soul and how it got there, you end up living in repetitive patterns of thought and reactivity without knowing why or knowing how to change. Most often, difficult situations that provoke quick and troubling reactions have little to do with the moment at hand. Instead, the reactions are caused by long-held beliefs and self-protective strategies. If underlying patterns remain unaddressed, they will continue to be repeated and become an excuse for "just the way I am," as if you can't change. Without looking at the source of those unwanted reactions, it's difficult to choose a better, slower response. Also, without identifying the roots of reactivity, it's difficult to receive the healing power of Jesus and develop new and more fruitful beliefs and responses.

The nine Enneagram type structures are examples of habitual patterns of reactivity that have developed and been reinforced through repetition. Rather than just accepting your dominant Enneagram pattern with all of its characteristics, it's important to be curious about *how* those patterns were formed. For instance, what false beliefs, fears, and binding reactions spring out of your early childhood experiences and perceptions? It's not enough to merely name a childhood wound if you wish to move *from* being reactive *to* being responsive. You need to look below the surface and prayerfully discover the starting point for subconscious patterns in order to be set free from them.

Some good questions to ask as you consider your own Enneagram pattern are: What experiences from my childhood set this type of pattern in motion? What is my earliest memory of feeling this way? What have I come to believe about myself that triggers an overreaction in my current life? What would it be like not to feel this way? What could replace the false narrative belief so I can respond differently?

For instance, Teresa identifies with Type One on the Enneagram, thus explaining her quick impulse to condemn herself if she makes a mistake. She came to realize how this pattern of needing to be perfect was established early in her life. She received award after award at every end-of-year school assembly. Her grandparents showered her with praise for her academics, but then they left. Her brother was difficult, so she had to be the "good child." When she excelled, she got attention; when she didn't, she felt dismissed. So, naturally, over time and through repeated experiences of reward and punishment, she came to believe "I have to be perfect to be worthy of love and attention."

As Teresa has allowed God's healing touch into her painful story, she's been learning not to be so hard on herself and to trust that people are not going to cut her off if she makes mistakes. She's learning to trust that God will not reject her, and will never leave or forsake her. Teresa has become less reactive and more responsive to whatever situations arise, regardless of whether or not she meets her standards of perfection, or if others notice her imperfections and emotions. She is also able to laugh at herself more. At the end of one of our times together, she told me that she now humorously sees her inner reactive critic as one of those chattering-teeth toys, and she imagines that Jesus is standing on top of it to shut it up!

Let's look at the other Enneagram patterns with a curiosity about possible sources of habitual reactivity. Twos need to consider how they came to believe they have to meet everyone else's needs and ignore their own. Threes might look at how they came to attach accomplishments to their self-worth. Fours could identify the genesis of feeling that something is inherently wrong with them. Fives could examine the root of their fear of being depleted. Sixes might look back to understand why they anxiously prepare for all possible contingencies. Sevens could face how their hunger for endless activity stemmed from childhood hurts. Eights might examine what drove them to be tough and invincible. Nines could identify why they believe they should go along with others to avoid relational discomfort. These are just a few examples of how "mining memories" will help us understand the habits of reactivity that often flood our present lives.

Patterns Used Against Us

Our son-in-law, Ryland, is an avid hunter. He grew up hunting with his dad, and now Ryland fills his own family's freezer with meat from his annual expeditions. He explained to me what is known as "patterning" in the hunting world. Animals are habitual; their daily routines of walking, feeding, and finding water usually follow the same path, and they generally remain within a certain radius. This makes it easy to track them if you know what to look for, like noticing the antler felt rubbed off on trees by the bucks. Once hunters locate the desired animals in an area, they use disguises and tricks, like different calls or scents, to lure them out into the open. The methods used will be different for each type of animal, depending on their established pattern of behavior and what attracts them. "We study their patterns so we have the greatest advantage over them—to find them, track them down, and get them before they see us," he told me.

As I related before, we are all creatures of habits and patterns. And we have an enemy who is described as a thief who seeks to kill, steal, and destroy us so that the image of God we are meant to reflect is negated (see John 10:10). The apostle Peter described this enemy as prowling "like a roaring lion looking for someone to devour" (1 Peter 5:8). We are being "hunted," and the hunter observes our patterns, our places of weakness, and our ingrained false beliefs, and "lures us out into the open" to distract us and take us out. The habitual patterns of our Adapted Self are prime targets for attacks from the enemy, usually disguised as an "accusing voice" or as the tone of our self-oriented temptations, all material for our overreactions.

I began to notice a pattern in my own life of becoming quite anxious about buying gifts—gifts for Christmas, birthdays, weddings, baby showers, and any gift-worthy occasion. I felt paralyzed; it was always a struggle to make a final purchase. My mind would swirl with questions about what someone might want or need, what they already had, and whether or not they would like what I'd bought. I've always wanted to give gifts, but I would become tense with fear whenever I set out to buy them. I didn't like just giving money or a gift card, but it was often the easy way out of my fretful state.

I began to wonder why I suffered from such an unsettling reaction about buying presents, so I brought it up with a spiritual director. She asked if I had any childhood memories about choosing gifts. A strong memory flooded my mind. I had given my best friend a Christmas present when I was about five years old. It may have been the first time I had picked out a gift on my own. I chose a musical jewelry box with a dancer that twirled when the lid was lifted. In this memory, I remember her opening the package and me sensing that she didn't really like it. I also recall an implication from her mother that I didn't know how to buy very good gifts. I don't know if this is true, but that was my perception. It stung, and I felt stupid and embarrassed. The limiting belief that I don't buy good gifts was lodged into my psyche, and the pattern of being bewildered about buying presents carried over into my adult life. Many years later, the simple act of purchasing gifts was still influenced by my experience as a five-year-old. Other scenarios along the way, like people asking for receipts to return gifts I had given them, reinforced this long-held belief. The "hunter" used this memory to relentlessly accuse me of being incompetent, oblivious, and unable to make a simple decision about a gift, thus paralyzing me in this particular way.

The director invited me to imagine Jesus in the memory with me. I saw Jesus holding the jewelry box, lifting the lid, and smiling as He watched the ballerina dance. The director then asked if Jesus said anything. I heard: *"This is a beautiful gift. You buy good gifts."* Then a flood of memories arose of some great gifts I've given, including the ideal present I had purchased for my grandson that week. I felt immediately restored and rejuvenated in my spirit.

I can't say I'm completely confident yet about purchasing presents, but I don't react or fret about it nearly as much. I tell myself the truth that I'm able to buy good and creative gifts, and whether the person likes them or not is less of a concern. I now consciously interrupt the pattern, not allowing the enemy to accuse me. You too can learn to interrupt your negative patterns and perceptions, and to quiet the accuser who seeks to paralyze and derail you.

Patterns for Creating Something New

I love to sew. I started when I was about ten years old, making Barbie doll clothes that I designed myself. I gleaned a lot from my mom and grandmother, who were both great seamstresses. Over time, my sewing skills improved, and my enjoyment of sewing grew still more when I took a sewing class in junior high. There, I learned how to follow a basic pattern, make adjustments, and put all the pieces together to create a garment. As an adult, I took classes on tailoring, pattern design, and professional clothing construction. This hobby developed into sewing clothes for myself and my children. I even made Jeff a powder blue leisure suit back in the day when they were popular; it looked very stylish with his white patent leather shoes! (I'm not surprised this fashion fad has never resurged!) I eventually co-owned Shear Joy, a sewing business I operated for several years with my dear friend Vicki.

An essential part of sewing is having a pattern to follow. Catalogs at the fabric store are full of patterns for everything from wedding gowns to home decor. When I want to make something, I peruse the catalogs to find ones that most align with what I intend to create. If it's a pillow, I can make dozens of them with the same pattern. When I've sewn bridesmaid dresses, I've used the basic pattern but then adjusted it to fit each woman.

How does sewing and following patterns apply to the shift *from* being reactive *to* being responsive? It's important to consider the models we follow and choose ones that result in fashioning how we want to live and respond. We have many options: the pattern of the world, of other people, of systems, of religions, of the current culture, many of which create heightened reactions, rather than thoughtful responses. It's easy to unconsciously follow any number of patterns, so we need to be wise and discerning about the ones we select. For instance, emulating the patterns of wise and godly mentors and teachers will guide us along our path to spiritual maturity. Also, what we read and what we watch will give us either life-giving patterns or soul-killing trends, so we need to be selective and careful about our exposures.

Better than any other option is the perfect pattern we've been given to follow: Jesus. Romans 8:29 tells us we are destined to be conformed to the image of Jesus: "For those

God foreknew he also predestined to be conformed to the image of his Son, that he might be the firstborn among many brothers and sisters." We were created to be like Jesus, act like Jesus, love like Jesus—in our own unique way. This is in contrast to the warning in Romans 12:2 to not be conformed to the pattern of the world.

Here are a few more passages about Jesus being our pattern to follow: "In your relationships with one another, have the same mindset as Christ Jesus" (Philippians 2:5ff). "Whoever claims to live in him must live as Jesus did" (1 John 2:6). "As I have loved you, so you must love one another" (John 13:34). "The student is not above the teacher, but everyone who is fully trained will be like their teacher" (Luke 6:40).

We can look at a full catalog of scriptures to find many, many "Jesus patterns" to follow and fashion our lives around, some of which we'll explore in the following chapters. But, for the theme of this chapter, how does following the pattern of Jesus help us become *less reactive* and *more responsive*? I propose that Jesus embodied two postures that indicate His responsiveness: *attentiveness* and *receptivity*. This was demonstrated by how He turned toward His Father and listened with openness and willingness. He responded by doing what He heard. He paused and went away to be alone and pray regularly. He wasn't in a hurry, but was attuned and responsive to the specific needs of the people around Him. He was attentive and available in the present moment, and, at the same time, lived out His holy eternal calling with focus, power, and love.

Receptivity and attentiveness are postures we too can develop by fashioning our lives after these patterns of Jesus.

As we are drawn to the center of our life with God, we will change *from* being reactive *to* being responsive. This will involve exploring the underlying sources of habitual patterns so we can pause, interrupt, and reframe our reactions, and make more thoughtful, peaceful, and sometimes courageous choices. It will also involve recognizing that the enemy of our souls capitalizes on our ingrained patterns and false beliefs in order to derail us and cause us to overreact. This awareness gives us power to address the false and accusing narratives with truth and confidence. And, lastly, this journey will involve developing a more attentive and receptive posture, like Jesus—to God, to ourselves, to others, and to our life circumstances. When we do, we will no longer be dominated by knee-jerk reactions that disrupt our well-being, our relationships, and our calling in the world. Instead, we will enjoy a more responsive and reflective life that radiates the fruit of the Spirit out from the core of our Authentic Self: love, joy, peace, patience, kindness, goodness, faithfulness, gentleness, and self-control.

CHAPTER 9

From Bondage *to* Freedom

Where the Spirit of the Lord is, there is liberty. Not liberty for license or to turn the benches upside down and to make a lot of noise. But liberty from the bondage of the law—liberty from the old covenant. Liberty to be the unique expression of Christ that He created you to be.

—JUAN CARLOS ORTIZ, *LIVING WITH JESUS TODAY*

As frightening as relinquishment sounds, the result is spiritual freedom—the freedom to be what and who God is calling me to be—not who I have been unconsciously programmed to be, who others are telling me to be, or even who I am determined to be. This is our true self in God, totally abandoned to the One who loves us.

—RUTH HALEY BARTON, *INVITATION TO RETREAT*

I really like playing board games, especially when our extended family gets together. Not everyone is enthusiastic, but they'll usually humor me and agree to play. And I really like making sure everyone understands the rules, so I go over them every time we begin. When a questionable move happens or there's any dispute about the game, I'll be the first to grab the instructions and read them out loud. The rules are there for a reason; they tell us how to play the game. But the rules aren't the reason we play; we play to be together, to enjoy each other, to have a shared experience, and to engage in a bit of fair competition (and win once in a while). If we just sat down and focused on the rules, we would miss the whole point of playing the game. In all honesty, I can be too uptight about the rules, and can ruin all the fun if I'm obsessed with making sure the rules are followed precisely to my satisfaction.

"Uptight rule keepers" were a focus of the apostle Paul's passionate letter to the Galatian church. He was pretty fired up and frustrated with the followers of Jesus who were being influenced by a group known as the Judaizers. These "rule keepers" were contradicting Paul's message of grace by insisting that true believers in Jesus should adhere to the rules and regulations of the Mosaic Law, especially circumcision, as proof of their faith. Essentially, the Judaizers taught that having sincere faith in Christ was not enough; to be truly "in," you had to follow the prescribed requirements. They were focused on the rules of the game—the Law—and were missing the joy of a Jesus-centered relationship by adding stipulations to the freedom the new believers in Jesus had been experiencing.

Paul's language is pretty harsh toward the Galatians at times, calling them "foolish" for being tricked into believ-

ing something contrary to what they believed when they
first received the Spirit of Christ. He challenged them with
these questions: "After beginning by means of the Spirit,
are you now trying to finish by means of the flesh?" (3:3),
and "How is it that you are turning back to those weak
and miserable forces? Do you wish to be enslaved by them
all over again?" (4:9). You can almost hear him vehemently
shouting, "What is wrong with you people? Don't you get
it?"

Why is Paul so upset? As a devout Jewish man, he knew
firsthand the bondage of having to meet the standards of
the Law to secure his standing with God and others. When
Christ was revealed to Paul by the grace of God, he was
overjoyed to no longer be a prisoner to sin and the Law
(3:22–23). He became zealous for a new faith, one of grace
and freedom, and longed for everyone else to be free from
the burden of obeying the Law as a mark of one's true faith.
His passionate plea to his friends in Galatia is summed up
by his strong admonition to "Stand fast therefore in the liberty by which Christ has made us free, and do not be entangled again with a yoke of bondage" (Galatians 5:1,
NKJV).

A yoke of bondage? What does this really mean, and
how does it apply to our pilgrimage today? In many Bible
translations, the word "slavery" is used here instead of
"bondage." Paul uses the metaphor of slavery quite often in
his writings, particularly in Chapters 6 through 8 in Romans. It's a rough word choice; slavery implies servitude,
oppression, being owned, having no rights—something
many people have grievously suffered under, and something

we all know is wrong. But it's a fitting word to describe the power of our sinful nature and of "the Law" when improperly applied: they can control us, oppress us, put us into subjection, and weigh us down with burdens we can't bear.

Now, you may be thinking: *This issue of the Mosaic Law doesn't have anything to do with me. I'm not even familiar with the bulk of the old covenant laws, and circumcision is certainly not associated with following Jesus, so I'm off the hook here. I'm not burdened by the Law like the Galatians were.*

That might be true, but the reality, whether we realize it or not, is that we've all created our own internal laws, based on the "accusing voice" of our Adapted Self. This voice will sound like our own thoughts, like someone else's, like certain religious standards, or like the norms of the culture we live in—all telling us *who* we should be, *what* we should do, and *how* we should think in order to be loved, validated, and acceptable. The "accusing voice" grabs the instructions and reads the rules, especially when we don't live up to them. We are held hostage to false beliefs, fears, and numerous other "weak and miserable" principles that can dominate our hearts, minds, and bodies.

How did these internal laws develop? In our formational years, we interpreted messages and experiences through filters of pleasure and pain, love and rejection, security and danger, control and powerlessness, and then translated what we perceived into our own rules. Often these internal laws stemmed from an "if/then" transactional arrangement we observed. In other words, we received a reward or positive payoff for doing or not doing certain things, and we received punishment or a negative return in the same way. Our basic brain structure figured this out. In Dr. Jerome D. Lubbe's book, *The Brain-Based Enneagram: you are not A number,* he explains in detail and yet quite simply how our brains are wired to move "towards pleasure and away from pain" for survival and self-gratification.[1] (Lubbe's book is a fascinating read if you want to understand the Enneagram from a neuroscientific perspective.)

Although this is a natural aspect of being human, our Adapted Self eventually becomes a taskmaster, reciting and repeating the "rule book" for what we have to be and do in order to win at the game of life: to be worthy, loved, valued, seen, filled, secure, satisfied, protected, significant, and more. The "laws of our own making" trap us in a cycle of "if/then" thinking that keeps us from experiencing the freedom available to us in the center of our life with God. Here are some examples of insidious and oppressive ways the voice of the inner law might communicate an "if/then" belief system. You may recognize these as related to the nine Enneagram patterns:

"*If* you mess up, *then* you'll be rejected."

"*If* you don't sacrifice for other people, *then* you won't have friends."

"*If* you don't perform well, *then* you'll be nothing."

"*If* you are like everyone else, *then* you'll be forgotten."

"*If* you don't know the right answers, *then* you'll look stupid."

"*If* you aren't well prepared, *then* it will be your fault if something bad happens."

"*If* you stay busy, *then* you can escape painful feelings."

"*If* you don't act strong, *then* you'll be hurt."

"*If* you stay in the background, *then* you won't cause problems for anyone."

An example of someone who made up a specific rule for herself early in life is Monica. She shared her story with me during several of our spiritual direction conversations. Monica grew up in a small town and was a good student, talented, well behaved, and received a lot of praise and attention for being the ideal girl. This felt good and reinforced her desire to perform well. But some people were jealous and didn't like her *because* she was so good at everything. She remembers being chosen for the lead in a school play and finding out that another student's mother was angry at Monica because *her* daughter wasn't picked. Someone told Monica that people were threatened by her natural abilities. She didn't like being criticized and making others angry, so she made up a law for herself: "Don't shine too brightly. If you do, then people won't like you." This internal message stuck with her through college and into her active adult life, affecting how she showed up in her work and in relationships. She downplayed her abilities and tried not to be too special, staying "average" so others wouldn't be critical or jealous of her. In a way, she had fallen asleep to her own self and her desires. She began to realize how much this interior standard was impacting how she approached her new job and co-workers. She felt anxious and afraid to speak up. She hesitated to do a good job and perhaps surpass the level of work others were doing. Receiving praise for a job well done made her uncomfortable.

Monica was caught in a bind between wanting to succeed and holding back, likening this internal struggle to being on a seesaw. We talked a bit about a seesaw and the importance of the fulcrum in the center, a picture of God's steady and embracing love. "If I remember how much God loves me, it's all okay. I want to be in God's embrace, surrounded and fortified by it." After a season of enjoying her intimate life with God, Monica felt herself "coming back." She was more clearheaded and purposeful. As she released the fear of others being jealous or critical, she no longer took responsibility for their reactions to her. She was more freed up to bring forth her best self, making a significant contribution at work, and, as a result, was happier and more confident. She moved *from* the bondage of her internal rule that said to avoid standing out, *to* the freedom of shining brightly in all of her endeavors.

Stop for a moment and consider your own internal laws. What are some of the "if/then" rules you hold for yourself? Can you sense how these keep you from experiencing the freedom available to you when you turn toward God? What might it be like for you to move *from* bondage *to* freedom by letting go of your rule book and enjoying the grace-filled life that God has for you in the center?

Woven throughout his letter to the Galatians, Paul offers a pathway to the liberty he so passionately longed for his friends to experience, and that we can also experience: *By Faith. Through Death. Into Freedom. With Love. In the Spirit.* Let's look at each of these more closely.

By Faith. Crowds followed Jesus everywhere. One time, after Jesus had fed a multitude of people with a few loaves of bread and some fish, He left the area. But the crowds went looking for Him and found Him. After seeing the miracles Jesus had done, the people were curious. "Then they asked him, 'What must we do to do the works God requires?' Jesus answered, 'The work of God is this: to believe in the one he has sent'" (John 6:28–29).

These people echoed a classic human question: "What is required of me to deserve God's favor and to do the work God expects? What are the 'laws' I need to obey to be a true follower of Jesus?" We want a metric, a checklist, a way of knowing exactly what actions are needed to make the A-list with God. This also gives us grounds for boasting or taking credit if things go well for us. But Jesus told them, in essence: "All you need to do is *believe* in me, the one God has sent for you." The Greek word here for "to believe" is *pisteúō*. This is more than just a mental assent that something is true. It means to put your trust and confidence in something, and to be committed to it. In this case, Jesus is saying, "Put your trust in Me. I came for you. Having confidence and faith in Me is what is most important to God."

Paul echoes these words in Galatians: "A person is not justified by the works of the law, but by faith in Jesus Christ. So we, too, have put our faith in Christ Jesus that we may be justified by faith in Christ and not by the works of the law, because by the works of the law no one will be justified" (2:16).

But, just as the Judaizers tacked on religious actions to validate one's relationship with God, we've done the same thing depending on the religious culture that influences us. "You *must* have a quiet time every day." "You *must* go to church." "You *must* speak in tongues." "You *must* witness to strangers." "You *must* do this or not do that, or you will lose your salvation." "You *should* . . ." "You *should not* . . ." I'm not suggesting here that there aren't important guidelines and valuable spiritual practices that nurture our spiritual lives—of course there are—but our standing with God is not dependent on performing them in a certain way.

You may be wondering if this grace-filled life of freedom means we can do whatever we want and there's no place or need for any standards of behavior. Paul emphatically addressed this misconception. "What then? Shall we sin because we are not under the law but under grace? By no means!" (Romans 6:15). Here Paul was addressing another prevalent teaching called antinomianism, which essentially gave license to live however you wanted because of the freedom Jesus offered. Jesus Himself did not toss out the Law, but elevated it in Matthew 5:17–18: "Do not think that I have come to abolish the Law or the Prophets; I have not come to abolish them but to fulfill them. For truly I tell you, until heaven and earth disappear, not the smallest letter, not the least stroke of a pen, will by any means disappear from the Law until everything is accomplished."

So, what's the distinction between valuing and obeying laws and not being in bondage to them? In essence, we don't gain favor and relationship with God by adhering to rules, but those who desire to follow in God's way will endeavor to follow the principles and practices that bring glory to God and are expressions of His love and purposes. We also don't need to base our worth on the rules we make for ourselves, but can choose the ones that bring health and well-being to our lives and the lives of others. Living without any standards at all would be like playing a board game with no rules at all.

Through Death. The apex of Paul's letter is this profound proclamation: "I have been crucified with Christ and I no longer live, but Christ lives in me. The life I now live in the body, I live by faith in the Son of God, who loved me and gave himself for me" (Galatians 2:20).

This is the true gospel, the good news, plain and simple: *We're free because we're dead! We're free because the One we trust lives inside of us! We win!*

My beloved teacher Dorothea taught me over and over again about "the exchanged life." In our Bible studies and in her letters to me after we moved away, she always brought me back to the fundamental truth that our old life is dead and that Christ lives in us and through us. Her teachings have grounded me for many, many years—since the small holy gatherings with her in my home. Dorothea wrote a little booklet called *A Wonderful Exchange.* Here are a couple of quotes from this dear woman of God. I hope her words touch you like they have touched me:

> *We all know that salvation is free and that it is a gift of God. But to become invisible or go into the deeper things of God we must pay a price. Paul says, "I am Crucified with Christ." We must, by faith, reckon that we too died with Christ on the cross, then act accordingly in all parts of our lives.*
>
> *Are you willing to reckon self, in all its pettiness, dead so that you can have the supreme privilege of Christ living on earth again through you? Why not make the exchange, move into the Kingdom and let the power of that life take hold of you and work out all that God has for you? Jesus Christ has done His part— your part is to lay hold of your inheritance in Him. For it is "Christ in you that is your hope of glory."*

Catch what she wants you to know: You have the *supreme privilege* of Christ living on earth through *you*! How does this happen? *From death to life.* "For we know that our old self was crucified with him so that the body ruled by sin might be done away with, that we should no longer be slaves to sin—because anyone who has died has been set free from sin. Now if we died with Christ, we believe that we will also live with him" (Romans 6:6–8). How are we to respond to this great mystery and truth? "Count yourselves dead to sin but alive to God in Christ Jesus" (Romans 6:11). What an amazing truth!

Into Freedom. Through putting our faith in Jesus, our identifying with the death and resurrection of Christ, and claiming ourselves dead to sin and alive to God, we are *set free from* our sinful and false Adapted Self, because it's dead and has no power over us. We are *set free from* all the manifestations of self-absorption, self-defensiveness, and self-promotion. We are *set free from* having to earn God's love by following certain rules. We are *set free to* live as our true Authentic Self, because Jesus lives in us and we are in union with the Triune God in the core of our being. We are *set free to* manifest the fruit of the Spirit from the core of our being and to reflect the image of God we were uniquely created to experience and express. As stated in Acts 13:39, "Through him everyone who believes is set free from every sin, a justification you were not able to obtain under the law of Moses."

If we were to set up two columns on a piece of paper with the headings *Free from* and *Free to* and then went through all of the Bible, we would come up with a very long list of words for both columns. Many years ago, I created such a list for myself. I still have the list, written on the cute country-style stationery that was popular then. On my list, the two columns were *Dead to* and *Alive to*. On the first line I wrote "My impatience," and in the second column I wrote "His patience." On the next line I wrote "My hard heart" on the left, and "His soft heart" on the right. On the third line I wrote "My resentment" juxtaposed with "His forgiveness." Below is a similar kind of list with a few examples of the Enneagram compulsions; many more could be added. On the left, you'll see what each is *Dead* and *Free from*, and on the right, what they can be *Alive* and *Free to*.

Dead and Free from	Alive and Free to
the compulsion to correct and judge	be at ease, grace-filled, and patient
the compulsion to overhelp and intrude	be unavailable to help, rested, and caring for oneself
the compulsion to look good and boast	be focused on others, relaxed, and faithful
the compulsion to create drama and envy others	be balanced, content, and grateful
the compulsion to know everything and withdraw	be open to mystery, engaged, and generous
the compulsion to worry and be full of self-doubt	be calm, decisive, and courageous
the compulsion to stay busy and indulge in pleasures	be in the present, satisfied, and mindful of suffering
the compulsion to be tough and take revenge	be tender, forgiving, and trusting
the compulsion to dismiss feelings and be distracted	be focused, involved, and bold

As I mentioned previously, Paul's overarching plea to the Galatians is for them to "Stand fast therefore in the liberty by which Christ has made us free, and do not be entangled again with a yoke of bondage" (Galatians 5:1, NKJV). In other words, don't turn back to your old ways, facing away from God and being enslaved to your ingrained rules; turn toward Jesus, *come further in* toward the center of your life with God, stay the course, and you will live into true freedom.

With Love. "You, my brothers and sisters, were called to be free. But do not use your freedom to indulge the flesh; rather, serve one another humbly in love. For the entire law is fulfilled in keeping this one command: 'Love your neighbor as yourself" (Galatians 5:13–14).

Paul's words echo the words of Jesus when a teacher of the law asked Him to name the greatest commandment. Jesus replied: " 'Love the Lord your God with all your heart and with all your soul and with all your mind.' This is the first and greatest commandment. And the second is like it: 'Love your neighbor as yourself.' All the Law and the Prophets hang on these two commandments" (Matthew 22:37–40).

When we're released from the accusing voice of the law, when we put our faith in Jesus, when we count ourselves dead to sin and alive to God, and when we step into the freedom available to us, pure love radiates out from us—to God, to others, and to ourselves.

Our capacity to love others and ourselves increases when we're united to God's love and when we focus our lives on the first part of Jesus's greatest commandment: loving God with the totality of who we are. Love is generative. Love begets love. It multiplies. It does not run out. It's a mystery and a miracle. Loving God with our whole selves gives us the capacity to love others and ourselves with the same kind of love, the kind of love described in 1 Corinthians 13:4–7:

"Love is patient, love is kind. It does not envy, it does not boast, it is not proud. It does not dishonor others, it is not self-seeking, it is not easily angered, it keeps no record of wrongs. Love does not delight in evil but rejoices with the truth. It always protects, always trusts, always hopes, always perseveres" (verses 4–7).

It's impossible to love this way from the false, Adapted Self. The ego self, with its fears and defenses, displays just the opposite: impatience, envy, boasting, arrogance, self-seeking, lack of kindness, quick to anger, keeping record of offenses, holding a grudge, delighting in wrongdoing, rejecting the truth; it is deceptive, doubtful, self-protective, and discouraged about the future, and it gives up, and lives in fear. Ouch!

When we move *from* bondage *to* freedom, we will be empowered by God to love with Divine Love—freely, faithfully, fully, and fiercely, without any regard for our own small selves, which are already dead anyway.

In the Spirit. Paul brings up a tension we all feel—the conflict between our Adapted Self strategies and the true essence of our Authentic Self. We feel pulled sometimes, or quite often, in the opposite direction of the arrows that point toward God, the arrows in *The Drawing*.

We are tempted to indulge in what our sinful, egocentric nature wants to do as opposed to following what the Spirit within would have us do. Paul expresses this internal tug-of-war and the way to prevail with these words:

"So I say, walk by the Spirit, and you will not gratify the desires of the flesh. For the flesh desires what is contrary to the Spirit, and the Spirit what is contrary to the flesh. They

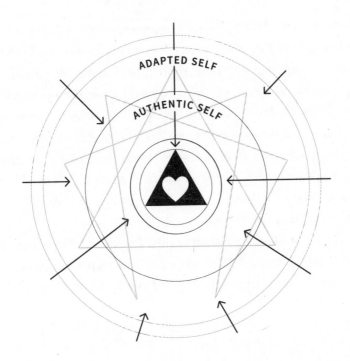

are in conflict with each other, so that you are not to do whatever you want. But if you are led by the Spirit, you are not under the law" (Galatians 5:16–18).

"Whoever sows to please their flesh, from the flesh will reap destruction; whoever sows to please the Spirit, from the Spirit will reap eternal life. Let us not become weary in doing good, for at the proper time we will reap a harvest if we do not give up" (Galatians 6:8–9).

Who wins the struggle between our dead flesh and our alive spirit? The one who walks by the Spirit, who is led by the Spirit, who lives by the Spirit, who keeps in step with the Spirit, and who sows to please the Spirit. Can it be any clearer?

Major W. Ian Thomas summarizes the victory of a Spirit-led life this way: "You . . . are called upon by God to *walk* by faith, to *walk* in the Spirit, resting the whole weight of your personality upon the living Christ who is in you; and as by faith you walk in the Spirit, so God declares you will not fulfill the lusts of the flesh. You will be liberated, emancipated, set free from the down-drag of that inbred wickedness, which Christ alone can overcome. You will be made more than conqueror through 'Christ who is our life'" (Colossians 3:4).[2]

By Faith. Through Death. Into Freedom. With Love. In the Spirit. These are the real "rules" for victory in the game of life, the rules that will lead us *from* bondage *to* freedom.

CHAPTER 10

From Wounded to Whole

If there is ever to be true healing and helping, a true sheltering and clothing for any of us, it is with nakedness and helplessness that it has to start.

—FREDERICK BUECHNER, *TELLING THE TRUTH*

I do not think that all who choose wrong roads perish; but their rescue consists in being put back on the right road. A wrong sum can be put right: but only by going back till you find the error and working it afresh from that point, never by simply going on. Evil can be undone, but it cannot "develop" into good. Time does not heal it.

—C. S. LEWIS, *THE GREAT DIVORCE*

Early one morning, Jesus was sitting in a courtyard ready to teach, as He did quite regularly. Suddenly, a commotion arose. A group of men were dragging a woman, barely clothed, through the crowd and right up to where Jesus was sitting, forcing her to stand in front of everyone. "Teacher, this woman was caught in the act of adultery. In the Law, Moses commanded us to stone such women. Now what do you say?" (John 8:4–5).

I love how Jesus responds. He didn't say anything, and I bet He hardly acknowledged their accusations. Instead, He bent over and wrote in the dirt with His fingers. In my imagination, I think He wrote something only the frightened woman could see: *Trust me. I've got this!* The men kept demanding an answer. Then Jesus stood up. He looked at them and then gave them permission to throw a stone at her if they were perfect examples of following the Law of Moses. Once more, He knelt and wrote in the dirt. He was so calm, cool, and collected. With Jesus still kneeling and focused on the ground, everyone started to leave, even the people who had been there to hear Him teach. Pretty soon, Jesus and the woman were the only ones left. At last, He stood up and spoke directly to her.

I'll get back to their conversation, but first let's consider how this woman ended up being an adulteress. At one time, she was a cute little baby and then a playful young girl, unwounded and innocent, full of hopes and dreams. When asked what she wanted to be when she grew up, she likely didn't answer "An adulteress." What changed? What led her to become the nameless "this woman"?

We don't know her story, but she certainly had one. Just like we all do. Was she wounded by rejection, neglect, or abuse? Was she lonely and longing for love and attention? Had she become poor with no means to support herself? Had she been told she was worthless or ugly? Or had she been praised for her beauty and sex appeal, but not affirmed for anything else? Was she competing with other women and looking for power and prestige? Regardless of the reasons, her true God-given identity was forgotten and buried beneath a wounded narrative and a fractured heart that landed her in the public eye, humiliated and fearing for her life. She was broken, wounded, and in need of a God-sized restoration to wholeness.

What Jesus said to her was remarkable: " 'Where are your accusers? Didn't even one of them condemn you?' 'No, Lord,' she said. And Jesus said, 'Neither do I. Go and sin no more' " (John 8:10–11, NLT). Can you imagine what she was expecting to hear from this well-known teacher of God's ways? Condemnation? Judgment? Rejection? More wounding messages? Jesus surprised her. He looked her in the eye, asked her where her accusers were, and she told Him there were none. He didn't scold her, ridicule her, or abandon her. Instead, He lovingly and graciously told her to go on her way and to stop living the way she was living.

Jesus offered her freedom from being controlled and condemned by the "accusing voices" that probably haunted her mind and heart most of the time, not just the accusers in this incident. Jesus told her to "sin no more." The Greek meaning of "sin" here is "missing the mark." In other words, Jesus communicated, *Don't keep missing the mark of your true identity and purpose in life. You weren't created to live this way; there's so much more for you!* He not only rescued her from death, but also gave her back her dignity. Jesus offered her hope that she could be different and live differently, no longer trapped by the pattern of false inner beliefs and bad choices stemming from earlier wounds. Jesus restored her and gave her a chance to become the person she dreamed of being. We don't know any more about her and how she responded to this new chance at life. Maybe she listened to Jesus and maybe she didn't. I like to think she was sitting in the crowd the next morning, with her head held high, her heart made whole, and her mind eager to learn from the One who had shown her such love, forgiveness, hope, and restoration.

The presence and voice of Jesus intervened, redeemed, and healed many, many people while He walked on the earth. The Gospels are filled with stories of times when Jesus spoke and people were healed not only from physical maladies, but from internal, spiritual brokenness too. Think of Zacchaeus, the hated tax collector who repaid people after meeting Jesus; the woman at the well who told her entire town about Jesus; the man who was delivered from a demon and restored to his right mind; and the prostitute who interrupted a party to anoint Jesus's feet with very expensive perfume.

Jesus is still in the business of restoring people to wholeness through the presence of His Spirit in our world and within us. I haven't witnessed too many miraculous physical healings, but I have known and observed healings of inner wounds for myself and for others. This chapter includes some stories of restorative moments for myself and for people I've worked with who've graciously given me permission to share a glimpse of their journey *from* woundedness *to* wholeness.

Before you read their stories, you may wonder how inner healing is even possible for *you*. You may ask, "How can I be healed and made whole given the difficult and damaging wounds I've experienced and the brokenness I feel?" As I mentioned in Chapter 8, the exciting and evolving discoveries of neuroscientists are revealing more and more about the miraculous neuroplasticity of our brains, which allows them to adapt and form new neural pathways when new information is introduced. Aha! God designed our bodies with the capacity to be renewed in our minds and hearts! The various methods of inner healing I've studied and experienced are based on this reality: we can become more *whole-minded*, *whole-hearted*, and *whole-bodied*. We don't have to keep carrying the heavy bricks of limiting beliefs and destructive patterns. We don't need to stay stuck in the regretful cycles of shame, fear, and anger that reside in certain neural networks of our brains. The inner messages that developed during our formative years may still influence our reactions, behaviors, attitudes, fears, avoidances, and interpretations of current events, often below the surface of our consciousness, but they can be reframed into a different story with less impact on our current lives.

What I've experienced most often for myself and witnessed in my work as a spiritual director is the power that comes when the presence of Jesus is invited into a recalled memory, one that carries with it wounds and negative, damaging, untrue belief structures. When someone brings up a current situation of strife and struggle, I often ask if their thoughts, feelings, and reactions seem familiar. We then ask God to reveal if there's an associated memory, perhaps a former wounding experience. Often the memory that arises doesn't seem to have any apparent connection to the current situation. The response I most often hear is "This is weird. What came to me is a memory when I was only such-and-such an age. I have no idea how it's related." Through the process of prayerfully inviting Jesus into the memory, noting what He does, how He looks, and what He says, something usually shifts and the recollection of the memory changes and is reframed. This then impacts the present scenario that is causing so much difficulty, generally calming it down and removing the intensity.

Lindsey started to meet with me because she said it felt like her inner work had come to a precipice, a giant cliff that looked deep and dark. She felt like God was going to expose something in her or to her, but she didn't know what it was or if she even wanted to see it. What was most clear was the amount of inner rage she felt toward a few people close to her, most often without a concrete reason as to why she was so upset. Lindsey generally controlled her anger outwardly, but inside it felt like a powerful force that wanted to explode. She wanted to be free from this strong reaction, but didn't know how to stop it from bombarding her.

As we talked, she admitted that she had struggled with this most of her life. It seemed to stem from not having an available parent to nurture her as a child, something she had grieved but not associated with anger. Lindsey's father died suddenly of a massive heart attack at the age of forty-four when she was nine years old. Her mom never fully recovered and was depressed, hopeless, and at times suicidal. Her mom was unable to be the emotional and physical support Lindsey needed, especially as a young child who'd lost her father in such a tragic way. Lindsey was alone, afraid, sad, and angry, although she couldn't have articulated those feelings then; she was just a wounded young girl trying to survive in a confusing and uncertain environment.

Lindsey and I asked the Lord to reveal a specific memory from her childhood that typified her angry feelings. A memory surfaced, one she had previously remembered but hated to think about, because it felt so dramatic. When Lindsey and her mom were dropped off at their home, the friend who was driving sensed something about the way her mom had said good-bye. She parked her car and followed them inside. Lindsey remembers sitting on a striped sofa and watching this friend chase her mom through the house; it seemed like a game, but she knew it wasn't. Suddenly, this friend gave her a bottle of pills and told her to go and hide them. Lindsey ran into the backyard and dumped them out. Years later she realized that her mom had intended to kill herself that day by overdosing on sleeping pills.

I suggested to Lindsey that she imagine Jesus there with her and to describe what He was doing or saying. After some silence, Lindsey spoke up. "He's in front of my mom. I've always thought maybe Jesus was chasing her, but now I see He was out in front. This hits a very deep place in me." For much of her life, Lindsey has known, in her mind, that Jesus is with her, but she hadn't sensed that He was very engaged in her life, similarly to how she felt about her parents' care for her. She had come to assume that "Love is present, but it's passive."

However, in revisiting this memory, this time she saw that Jesus was very engaged on her behalf, something she really needed to know. "I see now that if my mom had succeeded, I would have been an orphan. Jesus sent our friend to intervene for *me*." This reframed the painful memory into one of comfort, knowing Jesus was there and out in front fighting for her. When we turned our conversation back to her current internal anger, she realized that her anger flares up when she feels that the people she loves, and who love her, don't take active steps in their own lives, like seeking help for depression. Because they seem passive, she doesn't receive the care she needs and wants in the relationship. "I want to be fought for. I want to be taken care of. I don't want to be left to fend for myself."

Lindsey had buried anger toward her mom because she was unable to fully meet Lindsey's needs as a child and adolescent. Lindsey now realizes that her mom did attempt to care for her, but as a child her mom's passivity and lack of attention were perceived as a lack of love. Lindsey had carried these wounds forward into her present relationships, and also in her attitude toward Jesus, who seemed so uninvolved. How did her anger change? "It feels satisfied somehow. And, knowing Jesus is out in front, fighting for me, changes everything."

Lindsey's background was very traumatic, and had established neural pathways of painful beliefs about herself and her childhood that followed her into adulthood. Her deepening relationship with God and the process of inviting Jesus into her memories have been healing and restorative. She has also engaged in psychological therapy to address the impact of her childhood experiences. I'm a firm believer in therapy and other forms of support, so what I'm suggesting here as a way to move from woundedness to wholeness is not intended as a substitute for receiving guidance and treatment from professional practitioners.

In my work as a spiritual director and in my own life, I've noticed some common themes that often seem connected to former underlying wounds: *fear, a distorted image of God, self-judgment, unhealthy relational ties,* and *harbored bitterness.*

Fear. Fear is a powerful emotion, triggered for a wide variety of reasons and situations. One thing I've observed for myself and others is that strong negative reactions are often activated when one of our deepest fears appears to be validated by a current situation, seeming to prove that the fear is actually true. This fear is something we don't want to believe or accept, and we will react against it. I'll explain, using two Enneagram types as examples.

One of the deep underlying fears of Type Nines is that they don't matter very much and that their contribution in the world is of little value, perhaps stemming from former wounds of being ignored. If you think about it, this is a sad and painful thing to believe about yourself, causing insecurity and self-doubt. So, when a Nine musters up the courage to express an opinion and they are then dismissed or criticized, this reinforces to them that their deepest fear is actually true: *I don't really matter.* The passive-aggressive anger of Type Nines is often tied to this—they react by seething inwardly or exploding outwardly at being disregarded.

Type Threes are concerned that they won't perform well enough to gain the admiration of others; one of their deepest fears is that they are without value unless they succeed.

Again, this fear was likely formed by past painful experiences, perhaps feeling ridiculed for failing. So, whenever they fall short of their goals or fail in some way, especially in the eyes of others, this affirms that their deepest fear of being nothing without a stellar performance is actually true. Of course it isn't true, but that isn't how they interpret it. So, naturally, they become riddled with frustration and panic when their plans for success are in jeopardy.

Paying attention to what puts us in a fearful state can help us uncover the deep underlying fears we hold. What is something you deeply fear is true about you, and can you see the association between this fear and your regularly activated reactions?

When Ben showed up for our spiritual direction session, he said he was very anxious about some decisions he needed to make in his role as a pastor and also for his young family. He was afraid of making a bad decision that would lead to dire consequences in the future. As we talked about these fears, he admitted that as a child he had experienced a lot of what he called "fear-dumping." What he meant was that his home environment was full of fear, and he sees now that he suffered from frequent night terrors and dark dreams as a result. His dad was usually very busy and overwhelmed with his career; Ben remembers him as an anxious presence who was worried about many things. What Ben remembers most is the pressure to prepare for a good future, and the fear of not being prepared. "I was afraid I would ruin my future if I didn't do the right thing and succeed." He recalled a day in junior high when he received a poor grade on his report card and feared the scolding he would receive from his parents, assuming they would accuse him of sabotaging his future opportunities. He remembered standing at a fast-food restaurant after school, looking out the window, and wondering where he would sleep when he became homeless because of his poor grade. His current anxiety about making wrong decisions was tied to these childhood perceptions and the underlying fear that his family's future hinged on whether he did the right thing and made the best possible decisions.

We paused and I suggested to Ben that he ask God to give him an image of his fears. "It's like I'm being sucked down into a drain, circling around, and then I'm in complete darkness trying to find someone or something." At this point, Ben imagined Jesus in the scene. "He switched on the light and revealed the falseness of it all. It's bright now." Ben imagined he and Jesus laughing together, realizing that the fear itself wanted to be more powerful than it was, and that "it was ridiculous; it was nothing." Ben saw that when the concerns of life try to suck him down the drain of fear into darkness, he could allow the light of Jesus in to dissolve the fears. Ben also saw the strong power of Jesus's presence in this scene. "I can trust Him to be there with me in my fears and to lead me when I see His authority and power."

A distorted image of God. A person's perception of God is greatly impacted by how one views one or both parents. "There is interesting research that finds a correlation between your relationship with your parents, particularly your father, and your initial view of who God is and how much we want a relationship with Him."[1] I have found this to be true for many clients as they seek to connect with God on an intimate level.

Ethan grew up in an evangelical church and longed to have a missional purpose in his life by using his love for music. However, the more he was exposed to some "shady stuff" going on in churches, the more he doubted the goodness of God. For a while, he didn't see a need for God, but began to feel a deep-down longing for something bigger than himself. Yet he just wasn't sure he could trust God, or that he would ever perform well enough to know God intimately for the long haul. It was at this time he contacted me for spiritual direction.

Ethan was making an effort to connect with God and had moments of inspiration and attraction, but he quickly doubted it would last, and would shut down inside. The message that played in his head was, *Don't ever celebrate too quickly—you're not there yet.* I asked Ethan if this was familiar to him. "Yes, it's my dad's voice. When I was about age eleven and played a musical piece for my dad, he told me not to celebrate yet because I had a long way to go before it was good enough to perform for anyone else. This was pretty normal. All I really wanted to hear was that he was glad to be with me." This was a wounding moment for Ethan. He also shared that he formerly felt closest to God when he was "influential" as a Christian, but now, he just wanted to have a real and honest relationship with God without needing to prove himself worthy enough to make it happen.

We paused for a few moments; then I suggested that Ethan listen for God's voice, and ask how God sees him. He was quiet for a few minutes. Ethan then spoke with a shaky voice: "I heard two words and I saw two pictures. God called me 'son' and 'friend.' God's arm was around me, and then I was on my knees in a very 'free' kind of way." I asked Ethan how that felt. "I feel comforted and honored, empowered and hopeful. I'm God's son and friend! These are relational words, not performance words. I'm not alone. It feels too good to be true, but it's all I've ever wanted to know." During our next time together, Ethan said knowing he was God's friend clicked something fresh inside of him, and he sensed a new partnership with God in a fun and liberating way.

Self-judgment. The presence of inner criticism surfaces quite often when people share their stories and struggles with me. It's often said that we're "our own worst critics." Self-judgment and condemnation simmer within us, and we often don't realize how much these affect and restrict us.

Joanne had always assumed that her loud and ever-present inner critic was God's voice, correcting her and keeping her in line so she'd always do the right thing. As she began to learn more about herself, she realized how much she was motivated by guilt and how quick she was to judge and correct herself. She also began to realize that God was not the one who held a checklist of "shoulds" over her; it was her own internal monitoring system. She admitted to me that she would pick up "the Law"—however she perceived it to be—and figure out the right thing to do so she could feel good about herself. When she made any kind of mistake, big or small, she would get stuck in a "thought rut" and obsess for hours over what she did wrong, and then fret over possible criticism from others. Mistakes made her feel like an "inadequate person" who would never be good enough.

I asked Joanne how this self-judgment had developed into such a strong voice inside of her. "I was the good child. I was watched and rewarded for doing everything right." Yet she recalled an incident when she was not very nice to her neighbors and said mean things to them. Her dad was very mad at her, telling her how disappointed he was, and that she was a bad girl and deserved to be punished. Joanne was devastated that she had been an embarrassment to her dad, and his comments hurt her. "I still feel like the little girl who doesn't want to go up against my dad or disappoint him. I don't ever want to get into trouble. I know my dad loved me, but there were standards." Joanne has always felt evaluated and that everyone expected her to be perfect, so she became her own evaluator.

I wondered if there was an image that personified her self-judging tendency. She thought of a character on the *VeggieTales* cartoon series, the Rumor Weed, that just kept getting bigger and bigger and would take over. The accusing voice for Joanne got harsher and more critical when she thought she had done something wrong, telling her, *How could you? . . . You need to . . . Be sure you never do that again*. Now, she catches herself more quickly when she notices that she's ruminating on a mistake she's made. She stands up to the "weed" and says, "No, we're not going there." She also uses the acronym CALM—Christ Always Loves Me—to counteract this pervasive weed. Joanne reports that as she's given herself more grace and has practiced quieting the inner critic's voice, her stress level has gone down, she's more in touch with herself, she can laugh at her mistakes, and she has the freedom to make a different choice besides going down the debilitating self-judgment road.

Unhealthy relational ties. The subject of "soul ties" is often explored in many inner-healing models. In general, this refers to invisible relational cords that connect us at a soul level to another person, which can influence us in legitimate and healthy ways (like with a spouse or a child), or in unhealthy and paralyzing ways (like with a former intimate partner or someone who wounded us). One step toward the journey to wholeness is to identify the soul ties that keep us bound up, often connected to past wounds and usually indicated by how much our thoughts, feelings, and actions are consciously and subconsciously impacted by them.

Gloria came to meet with me a few days before her mother was coming from across the country for an extended visit. Gloria related that she gets very triggered around her mom and was dreading the next few weeks of managing her feelings toward her. She shared that her mom quickly slips into a martyr role and that their relationship is pretty superficial, something Gloria grieves and wishes she could change. She said she often hears her mother's critical voice in her head, telling her what to do and how to be, thus igniting flares of anger, impatience, and feelings of inadequacy.

During this session, Gloria told me about a dream she recently had of being caught in a spiderweb with threads covering and entrapping her. I wondered if this might be related to her mom's upcoming visit. I explained the concept of "soul ties" and invited her to return to what she could remember about the dream, and to invite Jesus to guide her thoughts about it. What she sensed was the Spirit surrounding her and dissolving the spidery threads, wiping the entangling strings away from her. It felt like being released from her mom's wounding remarks and the pervasive expectations that had tainted Gloria's attitude toward her. We revisited the dread she was feeling about her mom's visit, and she said she felt much calmer and more confident, and was grateful that God's Spirit would continue to release her from the binding messages so she could enjoy her mom's presence more.

Quite often a soul tie is with a person you once shared an intimate relationship with, not necessarily in a sexual way, but at the least in an emotional way. Joyce noticed she was regularly arguing in her head with a former boyfriend, trying to convince him that her life turned out all right without him. She didn't understand why it seemed so important to prove this to her old boyfriend, but she wanted to stop this ongoing inner conversation. As we explored the nature of this relationship, she related that her memories were sometimes lovely, but were also entangled with regrets and hurts. I shared with her the impact of soul ties, and she quickly saw that this was part of the issue. As she asked Jesus to show her what to do, Joyce visualized that the cords attached to her heart and to the other person's heart were dropping to the ground and dissolving. She felt some of her hurts dissolving too. Joyce let out a big sigh of relief and then released him into God's loving care.

Harbored bitterness. The writer of Hebrews portrays bitterness as a poisonous root with disastrous outcomes: "Watch out that no poisonous root of bitterness grows up to trouble you, corrupting many" (Hebrews 12:15b, NLT).

I personally experienced a powerful inner healing in my life when I recognized that a root of bitterness had festered in my soul. One day while meeting with my spiritual director, I brought up the agony I felt at not being able to move past critical and unkind reactions toward a person in my life. She invited me to be silent and ask God to reveal the source of this disturbing difficulty. A powerful image came to me: that of a sharp surgical instrument, like a lancet, going down through my head and chest and all the way to my lower gut. It went straight into a "boil" there and pierced it open, releasing thick pus that oozed out all over my insides. I literally doubled over in pain like I had received a gut punch. As a result, I saw how I had allowed a past hurt from this person to fester deep in my soul, poisoning me in ways I didn't realize. The harbored bitterness had developed into a full-blown infection, a contagion I passed from me to this other person and likely to others. As I welcomed this invitation to inner healing, God slowly removed the poison, sutured the wound, and led me to eventually release the other person from my built-up resentment.

Jesus is in the soul-restoration business of healing our wounds and leading us to wholeness. His miraculous transformation work is much like Kintsugi, the Japanese technique of putting broken pottery pieces back together with gold-infused lacquer, resulting in a stronger and more beautiful piece of art. On the repaired object, the shimmering seams of gold highlight the once-broken places, thus emphasizing and redeeming the fractures rather than hiding them. In a similar way, Jesus will address the fears that paralyze you and turn them into courage and strength. Jesus will correct the distorted images you hold of God, and reveal His love and grace. Jesus will answer your self-judgment with words of affirmation and delight. Jesus will set you free from the unhealthy relational ties that hold you back. Jesus will break through your harbored bitterness and heal your wounded heart. On this pilgrimage to a more centered life with God, the Kintsugi kind of transformation *from* wounded *to* whole will restore you to a gleaming and priceless one-of-a-kind work of art.

CHAPTER 11

From Shakable *to* Unshakable

Therefore everyone who hears these words of mine and puts them into practice is like a wise man who built his house on the rock. . . . But everyone who hears these words of mine and does not put them into practice is like a foolish man who built his house on sand.

—MATTHEW 7:24, 26

The heart must be renewed by divine grace, or it will be in vain to seek for purity of life. He who attempts to build up a noble, virtuous character independent of the grace of Christ is building his house upon the shifting sand.

—ELLEN G. WHITE, *PATRIARCHS AND PROPHETS*

Jesus made a bold claim at the end of His famous discourse commonly known as the Sermon on the Mount. He promised that if you hear His words and act on them, you won't collapse when difficult and challenging storms crash into your life. To highlight His point, Jesus used an illustration that's easy to grasp. He contrasted wise and foolish homebuilders: one who builds on a solid, unmovable foundation, and the other who constructs on unstable ground. It's pretty obvious which method is prudent and which one is senseless. The first will likely remain intact and the latter will implode when strong winds and waves buffet it. This begs an underlying question for His listeners: Do you want to remain stable and steady through all of life's circumstances, or do you want to fall and cave in whenever storms and struggles arise? The obvious answer is a no-brainer; I would guess most people want to keep standing.

Yet, in reality, people fall, institutions crash, relationships crumble, and "houses" of all kinds fail to hold up under the stresses, pressures, and pains of life in whatever form they come. None of us are untouched by loss, illness, change, disappointment, relational angst, injustice, and unsettling world events that cause us sorrow and strife and threaten our sense of security. We surely witnessed the instability and fluctuating nature of world systems and structures when the global pandemic of 2020 hit. Nothing was impervious to the shifting sands of the spreading virus, rocking the whole world and leaving people in a shaken state of fear and uncertainty.

Jesus claims we can remain standing even when inevitable storms come—but how do we get there? How do we build a life that will not fall? As God draws us to the center, how will we move *from* troubled *to* tranquil, *from* unsteady *to* secure, *from* shakable *to* unshakable?

In the illustration Jesus offers, the underpinning of the house is the key. The wise person with common sense secures the foundation to an unmovable rock, something that can't be destroyed even if the house teeters and sways. In the case of the foolish person, a foundation is not even mentioned; the careless builder sets up a home on unstable ground with no foundation at all.

If you've ever built a sandcastle, you know the futility of constructing sand walls to withstand the changing tides; eventually you'll watch your work of art fill up with water and be washed away. A house built on sand won't stay upright when powerful storms arise, because sand is porous and permeable, with spaces for water to enter in and wash it away. Tides come and go, ebb and flow, rise and fall, and turbulence will cause the sand on a beach to shift and relocate, sometimes to a whole new area. In a similar way, building our lives on any external thing that can rise and fall with circumstances will not keep us secure and steady for the long haul.

At a deeper and more personal level, our false Adapted Self is built on the porous and permeable ground of self-absorption, self-survival, and self-promotion. Our ego-driven patterns are unreliable, movable, and fragile. When major disasters and minor disturbances threaten the insufficient structure of our crafted persona, our Adapted Self strategies will frantically try to rebuild a sandcastle; but when the next wave of trouble strikes, it will give way.

Jeff's family owned a small rustic cabin on the Toutle River in Washington State, where he spent most of his childhood summers. The two-room structure sat on a foundation of cinderblocks. The gentle, meandering river near their cabin was fed by snowmelt from Mount Saint Helens. When the mountain erupted in 1980, tons of volcanic ash, fallen trees, and mud surged down the river and devastated the area, leaving it unrecognizable. Several months after the eruption, we obtained permission to go and search for the cabin. We had slim hopes of finding it, but thought it would be an adventure nonetheless. Jeff had a general sense of where the cabin might be, and lo and behold, we found it! It was surprisingly intact, nestled between two tall cedar trees on the property. We pushed the door open and saw, to our amazement, that only a few small items had fallen to the silt-covered floor. It was rather eerie and left us wondering how this rustic cabin had survived the flood while other houses had been destroyed or swept away. It didn't make any sense until we noticed the "silt line" fifteen feet up on the two cedar trees. This could only mean that the backwater of the river had lifted the cabin up between the two trees, where it jostled in place until the water receded and the cabin settled back down. It was an amusing scene to imagine, and we chuckled that this wasn't exactly in line with the words of Jesus about building your house on a good foundation; cinderblocks can hardly be considered a solid one. Yet the cabin still stood.

Given that storms and struggles are inevitable and that we alone are inadequate for sustaining and supporting ourselves, how can we remain standing like this cabin? When the winds and waves of life disturb our very core and rock our sense of well-being, what will keep us from collapsing? How can we face the inevitable challenges of life with confidence and certainty, with unshakable fortitude and steadiness?

While pondering the words of Jesus about building an unshakable foundation, I thought about the two cedars that had held the cabin in place, keeping it from being swept away. The tree roots must have been very deep and substantial to have withstood the force and volume of the volcanic debris. Although this "cabin survival" story doesn't coincide with the same metaphor Jesus used, the principles are the same. Deep roots and solid foundations matter; they hold things in place. Living a centered and unshakable life requires secure underpinnings. I offer these two cedars as metaphors for the two essential steps Jesus mentions to establish a solid foundation: *hear My words* and *put My words into practice*. Both assure our capacity to withstand whatever threatens to throw us off-kilter.

One Tree: "Hear my words"

Jesus says, "Listen to me! If you do, you won't be shaken. I promise." Jesus often ended His teachings with words like: "If anyone has ears to hear, let him hear" (Mark 4:23). In other words, "Are you *really* hearing Me?" Wherever He went, Jesus was surrounded by people eager and curious to hear His teachings and to witness His miraculous healings. Many people took in His words, but did they *really* hear what He was saying? There's a big difference. Are you listening, and are you *really* hearing the words Jesus speaks to you?

Two Greek variations are used in the New Testament for the English word "word." One is *logos* and the other is *rhema*. In general terms, *logos* is a word spoken or written, and *rhema* is a word applied with specific meaning to a person. In the passage we're considering here, in Matthew 7, Jesus used the Greek word *logos*—*hear the actual words I'm speaking to you*. In John 6:63, He used *rhema*: "The words I have spoken to you—they are full of the Spirit and life." In John 15, Jesus used both Greek words close together: "You are already clean because of the word [*logos*] I have spoken to you" (15:3) and "If you remain in me and my words [*rhema*] remain in you, ask whatever you wish, and it will be done for you" (15:7). How does this practically apply to us and our ability to hear the words—both *logos* and *rhema*—of Jesus?

To illustrate the power of hearing both "words," I'll introduce you to a monthly "listening group" that I've been blessed to be a part of for the past ten years. The format we use is always the same: someone shares a scripture, we listen to it with our *logos* and our *rhema* ears and hearts, and then we listen to each other in the same way. We follow the steps in what is commonly known as *Lectio Divina,* or "divine reading." Each time we gather, we prayerfully hear the word of God (*logos*) together and then we each listen silently for God's personal word (*rhema*) to us. The scripture is read four times, and we pause between readings with no comments. The first time it is read, we take in the entirety of the passage. The second time, we listen for a word or phrase that catches our attention. The third time, we notice any feelings and impressions. And lastly, we listen for a personal invitation from God related to what we've heard.

Following the readings, we turn our attention to one person at a time for a set sequence of sharing and listening. The person shares what they heard and experienced during the readings, followed by a time of silence for them to listen more deeply. The person shares again if anything new arose during the silence. The rest of the group mirrors back to the person what they heard without interpretation or expansion. Then more silence, more sharing, and more reflection back to the person, ending with a brief prayer of blessing. It's a very simple process, yet very powerful and profound. The *logos* from the passage we hear is identical, but the *rhema* each person receives is unique and pertinent to them. I'm always blessed and encouraged by what the Spirit speaks to me during our time together, and also amazed at how the Spirit speaks to everyone else in a unique way. It's a beautiful way to listen and *really* hear.

This type of "hearing" is not limited to being in a group like this; you can use the practice of *Lectio Divina* to hear personally both the *logos* words of Jesus and the *rhema* words spoken to you by His Spirit in order to build your life on God's immovable foundation.

So, are you listening and do you *really* hear Him? And, do you even *want* to hear Him? That's a foundational question. Sometimes we don't really want to hear what Jesus says because we're afraid we'll have to change or we'll have to do something we don't want to do. This hesitation to hear His words will keep us from the life-sustaining truths He wants us to know. And we may need to change, but always for the better.

Another obstacle to hearing Jesus is that we're spiritually deaf. Why? I've had actual hearing loss for most of my life due to scars on my eardrums from frequent ear infections as a child. When I was gifted with some hearing aids that were set to the right frequency for my unique needs, wow! I could hear with clarity and crispness the sounds and intonations my damaged ears could never pick up.

One reason we're deaf to God's truths is that we carry internal scars caused by untreated "infections" in our lives. Our spiritual ears are plugged by fear, bitterness, unforgiveness, control, pride, stubbornness, hurt, wounds, and many other conditions. In order to set our "house" on a firm foundation, we need to dig down and replace the damaging messages, the false beliefs, the injuries to our souls, and the outcomes of choices we've made. I've already covered some ways that we could address these realities in other chapters.

Other reasons we don't hear Jesus is because we're immersed in the world's clamor, the world's value system, and the world's assault on our true identity as God's beloved child. The words of others and the internal accusing voice drown out the teachings of Jesus. Round-the-clock information, news, entertainment, and activities numb and distract us, making it difficult to listen to the Spirit above all the noise. And we don't take the time to listen, to pause and reflect, to read and hear both the *logos* and *rhema* words of the scriptures and the Spirit.

Jesus spoke about three reasons for not really hearing His words—for not having a good root system—and one result of truly hearing His words in the parable of the sower and the seeds in Matthew 13:19–23. "When anyone hears the message about the kingdom and does not understand it, the evil one comes and snatches away what was sown in their heart. This is the seed sown along the path. The seed falling on rocky ground refers to someone who hears the word and at once receives it with joy. But since they have no root, they last only a short time. When trouble or persecution comes because of the word, they quickly fall away. The seed falling among the thorns refers to someone who hears the word, but the worries of this life and the deceitfulness of wealth choke the word, making it unfruitful. *But the seed falling on good soil refers to someone who hears the word and understands it.* This is the one who produces a crop, yielding a hundred, sixty or thirty times what was sown" (my emphasis).

Good soil produces a good crop or a strong tree to hold our "house" in place. The good soil of our inner lives needs to be cultivated by hearing God's word (*logos*) and *really* listening to fully comprehend what it means for us personally (*rhema*).

Second Tree: "Put my words into practice"

Both builders in this parable heard the words of Jesus, but only one acted on them—the wise one with the unshakable house. To remain steadfast and strong for when storms hit, we need to put into practice what Jesus says. It's easy to become saturated with words, more words, and more words with no impact. *Blah, blah, blah.* In one ear and out the other. Doing what Jesus says will build strong roots that hold us in place regardless of what happens in our lives. Every time you put the words of Jesus into practice, your roots go deeper and will ground you more securely.

One of my favorite places to write is at a friend's cottage on Puget Sound. During one of my breaks, I walked the beach and noticed how every house had a bulkhead standing between the sea and the home. I asked my friend Martin for a lesson about the value of bulkheads, or seawalls, and how they're built. I learned that seawalls are designed to withstand wave activity and storm surges that could threaten the integrity of the home's foundation. If water is able to seep into the ground around the foundation, it would eventually erode or sink, and the house on top of the foundation would lose its bearings, slip, and likely collapse. Seawalls are very expensive to build. For a majority of the time, the cost to build the seawall may seem like a waste of money, since it's rare for a storm to buffet the house so much that the water would get under it. But, without them, a rogue wave could cause widespread damage and the resulting cost to repair and rebuild is not worth the risk. Martin also told me that only 25 percent of the structure is seen above the ground. The pilings holding it in place are dug very deep, and are supported by underlying rock in order to withstand the pressure. Sounds a lot like the example of the wise builder.

Putting into practice what Jesus says is like building a seawall. It means doing things that may not make a difference right away, or don't seem all that important. Practicing what Jesus says is like sending roots down deep into our souls so that when life's circumstances buffet us, our houses will withstand the pressure and remain intact. Practicing when life is easy, calm, and normal will prepare us for inevitable surges of debris that threaten to undo us. Practicing His ways means exercising faith. Practicing means interrupting ego-driven patterns and developing new patterns to hold us steady. Putting into practice the *logos* words of the scriptures and the *rhema* words of the Spirit means we won't completely collapse when life gets rough. Repeated practices form new habits and then they become more automatic, like creating "spiritual muscle memory." To remain steady, we need to do what Jesus says!

Jesus covered a lot in the discourse that is recorded in Matthew 5 through 7, and it contains enough to hear and ponder for a lifetime. He spoke practical and challenging words about what it means to follow in the ways of God. Jesus wanted people to know how to live and stay standing. Yet, He didn't just say nice fuzzy words so everyone would feel comfortable. He got down to the nitty-gritty of some sensitive topics and demanded an even greater adherence to certain practices than what His listeners were accustomed to in their familiar religious law. He covered conditions for being blessed and how to pray. He encouraged His listeners to find the narrow road that leads to life and to seek first God's kingdom and His righteousness. Most of what He said is counterintuitive to our natural responses to people and life, but He spoke with the kind of authority that amazed people. When He finished speaking and went down the mountain, people began to follow Him everywhere. They were drawn to Jesus because the words He spoke were "words of spirit and life" (see John 6:63). The Gospel accounts are filled with stories of lives that were changed when they chose to follow Jesus and to practice what He taught.

One thread that weaves through the teachings of Jesus is human relationships. If you read carefully through the Sermon on the Mount with this theme in mind, Jesus touched on many things we should do to have solid relationships. On our pilgrimage of life toward the center of an unshakable life with God, we need people, companions with whom we share mutual support and encouragement. Jesus is very practical here: Cultivate good relationships, He says. Forgive, be generous, reconcile, humbly serve, and go the extra mile. Don't hoard everything for yourself, but share with others. Stay faithful in your marriage and keep your promises.

When storms threaten to knock you down, it's the people in your life who will lift you up, stand by you, show up at your doorstep with a meal or needed assistance, and provide a soft place to land when times are tough. Relationships are critical, and you can cultivate them and keep them only if you invest and treat people well, like Jesus instructs us to. It's really up to you to make the effort. It's not how many friends you have, but the quality of your commitment to the friendships you do have.

During the week I was writing this chapter, a dear friend

was undergoing serious issues with her intestinal system and was hospitalized for over a week. I've known this friend for fifty years, and she's part of a larger group of friends that emerged out of my high school Young Life experience. Years ago, when we were all starting our families and spreading out to different locations, we decided to meet up every Memorial Day weekend for a reunion at the beach. We did this for about twenty years. We would cram our cars full of kids and gear, endure sleepless nights, handle temper tantrums and mitigate conflicts, orchestrate fun and games, laugh a lot, and engage in deep but frequently interrupted conversations. It was a lot of work to pull off and we were exhausted when we arrived home. But it was worth the effort. Since those early days, we've supported each other through the deaths of loved ones, challenges with our children, and health situations. We've celebrated the marriages of our kids, births of grandchildren, accomplishments, and retirements. This week, we joined together via texts to pray for our dear friend's illness, surgery, and recovery. I was reminded again of the value of investing in people. Years ago, when we started our reunions and endured the sleepless nights, we didn't know how much we would need each other over the span of our lives.

I'm also blessed by a weekly Tuesday morning call at 8:00 A.M. with my dear friend and former sewing partner, Vicki. We've been "meeting" like this for over twenty years, sharing our hearts and always pointing one another to Jesus. Our friendship and commitment to each other has stabilized both of us when life circumstances have tossed and thrown us in a variety of ways.

This is a fitting place to offer a tribute to my wonderful mom and dad, who demonstrated the value of people throughout their lives. They both volunteered in countless ways in our community, investing their time and resources in helping people. They nurtured lifetime friendships, often initiating connections with others. Both were named, at separate times, the Clark County "Citizen of the Year" for their selfless service and leadership. Even as my mom was dying, she made phone calls from her hospital bed for the annual poinsettia sale in support of a local nonprofit. During the writing of this, I organized my father's 100th birthday celebration. Since he enjoys staying in touch with old and new friends and family, the guest list expanded to over two hundred people—which says a lot, since many of his peers have passed away. The party was amazing, and my dad was elated to connect with so many dear people. Everyone remarked how kind and thoughtful he has always been to them; they felt the same about my mom. My parents proved out the principle that you reap what you sow. If you invest in people, treat them with a 1 Corinthians 13 kind of love, and serve without expecting a reward, you will enjoy a life filled with good relationships, and will be supported when you need it most.

Remember that the second tree that will keep us from being shaken is putting into practice the things Jesus said. Let's look at three instructions found in the Sermon on the Mount, ones that aren't naturally easy for us to follow, but are essential to putting our roots down deep.

1) *"But I tell you, love your enemies and pray for those who persecute you" (Matthew 5:44).* At a time in history

when we are so polarized, and living in a culture that is quick to tear down anyone who doesn't agree or who seems to pose a threat, what a revolutionary difference it would make if we adhered to this command to love our enemies and pray for those who hurt us. When Jesus said this two thousand years ago, the world was much the same; deep chasms in the political, religious, ethnic, and economic sectors also existed. So, I can imagine this was a shocking and uncomfortable statement for the people to hear from Jesus. They might have thought, *I don't know—maybe this is going just a little too far. Love my enemies? Pray for them? Impossible!*

This terse command doesn't apply just on a global scale, but in our private lives, in the nitty-gritty of the relationships we engage in every day. We all have people in our lives who are tough to love and we'd rather avoid. My friend Alexandra Kuykendall, in her encouraging book for our times called *Seeking Out Goodness,* asks this challenging question about the call to love and pray for our enemies: "How can we see God's goodness in the world if we're only willing to be in spheres where his goodness is reflected back to us in ways that feel palatable and pleasant?" Further, in reflecting on the words of Jesus here (which she quoted using the version in The Message translation), she noted: "If this isn't convicting, I'm not sure what it is. Jesus is telling us to grow up. Live like the kingdom subjects we are."[1]

When we actually pray for people we find to be challenging, our hearts will change and we can extend more love and grace because the love of Jesus can more freely flow through us. Once when I was part of a team organizing a large event, one of the other members was very controlling and rigid. I was quite annoyed and frustrated with him, and I spent a lot of time and energy venting about his behavior. I could hardly stand to be around him; my attitude toward him dampened my whole enjoyment of the work. He was not really my enemy, and I was persecuted only by my festering anger, but I still felt like he was against me. It occurred to me that perhaps I should at least pray for him. I did, even though at first my prayers weren't very sincere. But I was tired of having my mind dominated by this person. I also confessed my bad attitude and lack of patience. Without any dogged determination on my part to love him and treat him better, I just started to. It was a supernatural shift that I noticed almost overnight. By the end of the event, he became a good friend, we worked well together, and he was one of my favorite people on the team. I put into practice the words of Jesus. The roots in my tree grew stronger.

2) *"For if you forgive other people when they sin against you, your heavenly Father will also forgive you. But if you do not forgive others their sins, your Father will not forgive your sins"* (Matthew 6:14–15). When Becca arrived for our time together, she said she was flooded with a deep pain from broken relationships with people who were very involved in the original startup of their church. What triggered her current hurt was hearing about the successful endeavors of some of the people, leaving her feeling abandoned and alone. "They left me behind in the most difficult moments of getting the ministry of our church off the ground." She felt deep resentment toward them down in

her gut, and jealousy that they were doing well. It was as if they still had a hold on her somehow. We talked about *forgiveness,* and the fact that the Greek translation of the word implies a "sending away and setting free." I invited Becca to name each person and to imagine what it would look like to forgive them. In the quiet, she visualized saying goodbye and imagined watching them go over a fence while she gave them a blessing to "be free." She then felt free from the hurt and resentment that had built up inside of her. She recently reported to me that she has come around many times to forgiving others in the same manner. Becca became less shakable and her roots grew down deeper.

The verse quoted above, too, is a bit difficult to accept. Does it really mean that we have to forgive everyone who has injured us in order for God to forgive us? A very insightful interview with David Augsburger, a former professor at Fuller Theological Seminary, offers some helpful counsel on the issue of forgiveness. For instance, he cautions those who have been injured not to forgive prematurely, without an appropriate process. In regard to the verse above, Augsburger offers this perspective, which I find very helpful and hopeful: "Jesus recognizes that the stubbornly unforgiving heart closes itself to both giving and receiving—and he urges us to have a heart open to forgiveness. But taking time to work through the injury to regain the brother or sister, as Jesus teaches elsewhere, is what it looks like to take forgiveness seriously. It is not an unforgiving attitude to insist on the integrity of the process."[2]

3) *"And why worry about a speck in your friend's eye when you have a log in your own? How can you think of*

saying to your friend, 'Let me help you get rid of that speck in your eye,' when you can't see past the log in your own eye? Hypocrite! First get rid of the log in your own eye; then you will see well enough to deal with the speck in your friend's eye" (Matthew 7:3–5, NLT).

Have you ever criticized someone, both inwardly and outwardly, and mentally cogitated on all the ways they're flawed, how they should change, and how you could straighten them out? I sure have! This kind of "meditation" can take up a lot of space and energy in our minds and hearts, and leaves us shaken up inside. Jesus is telling us here to focus more on looking at ourselves and working on our own flaws, rather than wasting so much time fretting about the faults and shortcomings of others.

Many years ago at a conference, I heard an important principle along these lines that I've tried to put into practice; it's been very helpful, although not always easy. I believe it has prevented some of my relationships from breaking apart. It is this: Even if I think I'm only 5 percent at fault in a situation, my responsibility is to take honest ownership of that 5 percent, apologize without expecting any admission of wrong from the other, and leave the remaining 95 percent for the other to deal with in their own way.

In one such instance, I had to swallow my pride and confess my minor part in a major problem that had quite unfavorable outcomes due to the irresponsibility of one person. I had been relentlessly rehearsing conversations with this person in my head, talking way too much about her character flaws and mistakes with others, and holding on to my anger. Then I remembered this principle about addressing the log in my own eye, my 5 percent. I initiated a meeting and apologized for my critical attitude, for gossiping about her, and for an action I regretted taking when this problematic situation was developing. I then waited for her to admit how stupid and thoughtless her actions had been, to recognize the log in her own eye, thus giving me full satisfaction that she had taken ownership for her part. That never came, and I don't think she even realized she had done anything wrong. I had to take a deep breath, let it all go, walk away, release her from the speck in her eye, and enjoy better sight without the log still in mine. We have remained friends, and I look back at this difficult story with a sense of humor, and gratitude for the opportunity to practice what Jesus taught.

Listen, listen, listen to what Jesus says. Practice, practice, practice doing what Jesus says. He promises this is how we can stay the course through all the ups and downs, the trials and travails, the struggles and storms of our lives. I invite you now to read slowly through the Sermon on the Mount, paying attention to what catches your attention. Take in the *logos* words and also listen for the *rhema* words for you personally. Is there one instruction from Jesus that you can begin to put into practice?

You might think these instructions could be interpreted as ways to prove your worth, gain God's love, or live up to unrealistic expectations. But I think Jesus has something else in mind when He told us to listen and do what He said. I imagine Him saying, "Hey, I desire for you to enjoy a good life. It will get rough at times because life is like that. There will be trials and temptations, but I want you to keep standing tall even if you sway and falter a bit. You'll need a clear conscience when life throws you for a loop. You'll need to know how to choose wisely when the way seems unclear. You'll need good relationships for when times are tough. So I'm giving you some things to practice doing all the time. These will help you remain steady for the long haul. Listen to Me and act on what I tell you, even though it may not be your first impulse. I promise that your house built on My foundation will not fall. You will move *from* shakable *to* unshakable. Trust Me!"

CHAPTER 12

From Burdened *to* Rested

Come to Me, all you who labor and are heavy laden, and I will give you rest. Take My yoke upon you and learn from Me, for I am gentle and lowly in heart, and you will find rest for your souls. For My yoke is easy and My burden is light.

—MATTHEW 11:28–30, NKJV

The needy are those to whom Jesus has consistently addressed himself and for whom he is always there. . . . Jesus' invitation goes out to all those for whom life has become a grind, for whom existence is laborious, to those, in a word, from whom the juice has gone out of life and all that's left is the rind. Jesus' heart goes out to them.

—FREDERICK DALE BRUNER, *MATTHEW: A COMMENTARY; VOLUME 1*

Rest . . . Ahhh! What a promise! In the scripture above, Jesus extends an offer of rest to those who carry heavy burdens and are weighed down by weariness. This invitation feels like an all-expenses-paid trip to a remote tropical island with nothing to do but relax and play without a care in the world. Sign me up!

Yet it feels so unrealistic to just drop responsibilities and obligations, to take it easy and chill out when life is a struggle and so many things demand our attention. At first glance, we might interpret this invitation as a "Wouldn't that be nice?" escape, but Jesus is talking about a different kind of rest—a rest for the soul. What would it be like to truly experience such deep-down rest? As we turn our focus to the center of our life with God, how can we move *from* weariness *to* refreshment? *From* burdened *to* rested?

First of all, we need to admit we're actually tired and worn out. When Jesus offers this enticing promise of rest, He specifies who this invitation is for: *"all you who are weary and burdened."* Frederick Dale Bruner, in his excellent commentary on Matthew's Gospel, translates this phrase as "all of you who are struggling and carrying too much."[1] Does this include you? Do you even realize you're carrying more than you're meant to handle, not just in outward obligations, but inside your own self? So often, we just keep going, pressing on, without an awareness of the inner pressures we carry, the false narratives and inner self-talk that weigh us down, and the burdens we assume we must shoulder.

I'm reminded of a watershed moment when I was in my early thirties. I was adjusting to a new town while navigating life with our two active young daughters and pregnant with our third child. I kept up a cheerful persona in public, but behind the closed curtains of our home, I was depressed, angry, and frustrated. I felt lost and lonely without the props and people I had relied on for friendship, encouragement, and support. I was overwhelmed, the house was a mess, and I was short on patience with my family. I had usually been able to pull myself up by my own bootstraps, but my confidence, competence, and capacity had dissolved, and I flailed and floundered to make it through each day. I felt like a total failure and just couldn't see my way through.

Prior to our move, I was in a Bible study with Dorothea, whom I've already introduced. She was the godliest woman I've ever known. In our times together, I would listen, nod and agree, take notes, and absorb the truths she taught me. She spoke over and over again of the "exchanged life" and the "mystery of Christ in you." She also talked about the "Sabbath rest" available to us all day, every day, regardless of our circumstances. It all sounded fabulous and true and I "believed" it. I even taught it to others. I took it all in, said the right words, and was fully on board, without a doubt. But when I found myself in the pits of despair and with no reserves, the promises of Jesus seemed empty and beyond my grasp, and they certainly didn't match up to my very real existence. I was weary and burdened, and I felt no rest for my soul.

One morning, as I was putting dirty laundry in the washer, I found it full of wet and smelly clothes from a few days prior. Another sign of failure. I slammed the lid down and shouted in desperation, "Oh, God, I can't do anything right!" In the next moment, I sensed God say, "Oh good, you finally get it. Now I can help you!" A fresh realization hit me. Right then, all I'd heard from Dorothea became crystal clear to me; it wasn't just theory, but absolutely real. I immediately called Jeff at work and told him I had proven the Bible to be true, to which he replied, "Oh really?" I then rambled on with "Oh yes . . . it's all true. In my flesh dwells no good thing; I'm a sinner who is incapable of running my life; I need to come to Jesus; my only hope is His life in me; it's His life in exchange for my life; I get it, I get it!" I was elated to finally admit this reality and to know it deep down in my core. A liberating lightness and holy relief flooded my whole being. My soul felt refreshed and renewed, even though the everyday piles of laundry and responsibilities remained.

As I look back on this experience, it wasn't the daily demands of life that had made me so weary and defeated; it was the way I was carrying them. I was relying on my own resources to prove I was competent. I was hesitant to ask for help, and I was too stubborn and proud to admit I was struggling. I felt the heavy burden of trying to look good and "together" in the eyes of the people in our new town. I was striving on my own while Jesus was a nice afterthought. It wasn't until I finally admitted my desperation and incapacity that I was open and able to experience the true rest my inner soul was craving.

Until we come to the stark recognition that *we are struggling and carrying too much*, the rest Jesus offers isn't very accessible. We have to admit that we've come to the end of our rope, weighed down beyond what our own resources can supply. The invitation from Jesus is for those who have reached their limit, who are tired of pleasing people, who are working too hard to fulfill roles and expectations, who are exhausted from worry, who are disgusted with themselves, who carry burdens they shouldn't be carrying, and who feel the weight of perfection and control imposed by their own inner dialogue. As long as we think we can handle life on our own, we'll just keep striving and toiling and growing weary, without any rest in sight.

Once we concede that we're spent, we need to take a close look at what makes our souls weary and depleted. What weighs us down, leaving us tired and discouraged? Of course, it's easy to list the ongoing cares, challenges, and chores of our lives. But it seems Jesus is pointing to a much more pervasive weariness—an inner fatigue that prevents us from experiencing the "rest for the soul" He offers. Jesus is not addressing responsibilities and activities in our external life, although we need to assess our circumstances honestly and make changes if we are undergoing undue stress because of them. Jesus points to what drives us *below* the surface, in our inner life, in our subconscious, and how we toil and strive inwardly.

All of us face the ordeal of making our way in the world with all the limitations and pressures of being human. As we've talked about earlier, our Adapted Self structure has created standards and strivings that become onerous and impossible to reach, like our own set of "performance laws." It's as if we carry around an internal backpack filled with all of our survival and self-protection supplies as we wander through the wilderness of being human. Over time, our backpack becomes full of heavy bricks we've collected from wounding words, painful memories, experiences of rejection, dangers, accusations, misperceptions, sufferings, and losses. It's the truth of the human journey. Consider this: If we carry around an "internal backpack" loaded with heavy negative bricks we've accumulated, then our "soul space" becomes weighed down and weary, leaving little room for what could be life-giving and liberating.

The meaning of "heavy laden" implies that a load is put on something, like piling a ship with freight. In other words, those who need the rest Jesus gives are those weighed down by burdens and beliefs they've loaded on themselves or burdens they've assumed to be theirs. What have you loaded on yourself?

One way to identify the load we've taken on is to look at some of the compulsive drives of the Enneagram patterns, which can feel like internal taskmasters wearing us down. For instance, Type Ones judge themselves by standards of perfection they'll never reach. Type Twos assume the role of caretaker, but the needs of others never end. Type Threes strive to meet all their goals and keep adding tasks they can't complete. Type Fours try so hard to be unique that they forget who they really are. Type Fives panic at not knowing enough, so they work overtime to learn more. Type Sixes burden themselves with avoiding uncertainty and worrying that they won't think of everything. Type Sevens keep frantically moving to avoid feeling their own pain. Type Eights push to control their environment so they won't be ambushed. Type Nines take on the weight of everyone's expectations and fall asleep to their own desires.

Assumed burdens like these become like heavy bricks in our inner lives.

The beautiful invitation Jesus extends to those who know and admit they're weary and heavy laden is simply *"Come to Me."* The Greek word for this phrase is more than a casual invitation. It's an imperative and strong command, like "Come here to Me!" It's like a parent who firmly and gently tells an out-of-sorts child who needs to be calmed and comforted, "Come here to me *now*. Shh . . . quiet. Let me hold you. Be with me. It's going to be okay." Jesus commands us to come to Him personally, not just to ideas and principles about Him. To *come further in* to the One who sees, knows, understands, and loves us; to the One who implores us to "come and rest."

One day I met with Jada for spiritual direction and she shared how exhausted she was by all that was happening in the world and how discouraged she felt about her own calling to make a difference. She had been working so hard, but was now weary and felt like giving up. She mentioned how easy it was for her to abandon her regular life-giving rhythms and stop by her favorite store for her favorite cookie to satisfy her angst and fatigue. As we sat in silence with God, she imagined herself sitting on a bench in the dugout of a softball game. While watching her team on the field, she had no energy or desire to get back in the game. She was hoping they would win, but she could hardly even cheer them on; it all seemed so futile. As she invited God into this imagined scene, Jada sensed a loving presence behind her and a hand patting her on the shoulder, saying,

"You just sit here and rest awhile." It was like a coach giving her a needed break, and it was such a welcome reprieve from all of the stress and strain she felt.

Implicit in Jesus's invitation "Come here to Me" is *Don't go somewhere else to get what you need.* How quickly we employ other ways to ease our troubles and numb our stresses. We run to other people, we pack our schedules, we buy more stuff, we engage in distracting activities, we eat comfort food, pour a few drinks, binge-watch, scroll through social media, take drugs, harm our bodies, look at pornography, and on the list goes. Not all of these are bad or wrong, but some do have harmful long-term effects and are evil temptations. Regardless of what outlet we choose to ease our weariness and lessen our load, all options provide a temporary reprieve from our troubles, but can never fully satisfy the deeper longings and needs of our souls like the rest Jesus offers.

The word "rest" is mentioned twice in this passage— "I will give you *rest*" and "you will find *rest* for your soul." Rest is given and rest is to be found. The Greek word for the first phrase is *anapauo,* meaning "to give rest, to give intermission from labor."[2] A longer definition from the *Blue Letter Bible* is "to cause or permit one to cease from any movement or labor in order to recover and collect strength." Like the coach in Jada's imagined prayer, Jesus is saying, "Come here, rest with me. Stop working for now. You don't need to keep toiling to carry the heavy burdens you think you have to carry. Trust me; you'll recover and be strengthened once you receive the refreshment you need."

I really like the word "refreshment." It feels like a cold

drink on a hot day. Like a full night's sleep. Like a warm cup of chai tea on a wintry morning. Like a resolved relationship after a conflict. Like a delicious dinner and a relaxing conversation with those you love. When we experience this type of refreshment, we often say, "I really needed that!" Refreshment does one's heart, mind, and body a world of good, and makes it possible to keep going.

How does Jesus give us true and lasting refreshment, the needed "pick-me-up" for our weary souls? Many incidents are recorded in the Bible of how Jesus took time away to pray and be alone, how He slept in the bow of a boat during a storm, how He was tired and sat down by a well, how He carried out His divine calling with a steady and seemingly effortless manner. We can hold Him up as the pattern to follow and adopt habits to emulate His actions, but it's even more than that. The rest Jesus gives radiates out from the very life of His Spirit within you. The divine state of rest *in you* is the true and only source of refreshment for your soul. It's the "exchanged life" that Dorothea taught me about. It's a divine mystery, and it's yours for the taking. Jesus, by the Spirit, is at rest in the midst of your worries and shouldering the weight of your toil and troubles even if you don't recognize it. It's how you can come to Him: He is right there, inside of you, in union with your spirit in the center of God's love. Jesus is not striving, and He gives you the rest you need with nothing to prove and nothing to do but "Come."

The Greek word for the second mention of "rest" is *anapausis*, very similar to the first. According to *Vine's Expository Dictionary*, as quoted on the *Blue Letter Bible* website, the word used here is the same word in the Old Testament for "Sabbath rest," which I will come back to later in this chapter.

This second use of the word "rest" is also combined with "will find," which means "to come upon, hit upon, to meet with; after searching to find a thing sought; to fall in with; to see, learn, understand, discover, detect, come to know."[3] In other words, when you come to Jesus with your burdens, you begin to realize you're actually feeling rested, you're at peace, you aren't striving so much. Ahh . . . the true rest is just there for you to "fall in with" and experience by accepting the invitation from Jesus to come and find the rest He gives.

Another person I met with for spiritual direction described her present circumstances as similar to the plight of Jesus's disciples in the middle of a storm while Jesus slept comfortably on a cushion (Mark 4:36–38). She said, "My boat is swamped, the waves are crashing all around me, and I want to shake Jesus awake and scream at Him, 'What is going on? You need to do something!'" As we talked more about this story and her life, I wondered if there was another option for her besides shaking Jesus awake. She replied, "I really just want to curl up and fall asleep too." She then imagined herself finding a comfortable spot near Jesus to lie down and relax. Jesus put His arm gently around her and said, "It's all okay. Just stay here with Me and you'll find the rest you really need."

Rest given. Rest to be found. How can we know this deep-down kind of rest? In between these two phrases, Jesus gives us two instructions, the "how-to" for moving *from* burdened *to* rested: *"Take My yoke upon you, and learn of Me."*

"Take my yoke upon you"

It's interesting that Jesus used "yoke" as a metaphor when speaking about rest. To be yoked together with something is to be coupled with it, to be bound with it in order to get some work accomplished, like two work animals attached to a plow and controlled by a driver to make them pull it. As Bruner explains, "A yoke is a work instrument. Thus when Jesus offers a yoke he offers what we might think tired workers need least. They need a mattress or a vacation, not a yoke. But Jesus realizes that the most restful gift he can give the tired is a *new way to carry life,* a fresh way to bear responsibilities"[4] (italics mine). And Bruner further states, "A yoke is not a sitting instrument; it is a walking instrument . . . As we seek to live in obedience to Jesus, we learn from Jesus along the way."[5]

In other words, when we come to Jesus and "sit in the dugout" or "rest in the boat" and experience the refreshment He gives, it doesn't mean we stop working. Jesus encourages action, but in a different way than we normally carry our load. His invitation to us might sound like: "Now that you've rested a bit, rise up and lift My yoke around your neck. It's time to work again, but now pair yourself with Me. Walk with Me. Work with Me, not by yourself. And, as we go, you'll learn how to live in a more rested way. I'm a humble and gentle teacher, not a harsh and demanding one. I won't burden you with rules and demands and expectations. *Come here to Me*—let Me take off your backpack. It's too much for you to carry. Let's shoulder this together, in step with each other. Then your burdens won't be so daunting, and you won't be so weary."

Jesus says to take *His* yoke upon ourselves, not our version of the yoke we've placed on ourselves to plow through life. What was His yoke, His work to do, His burden? First of all, Jesus says His yoke is easy and His burden is light. When we study His life, we see the yoke He took up and how He carried it out. As recorded in Luke 4:18–19, Jesus described His yoke this way when He proclaimed this in a synagogue:

> *The Spirit of the Lord is on me,*
> > *because he has anointed me*
> > *to proclaim good news to the poor.*
> *He has sent me to proclaim freedom for the prisoners*
> > *and recovery of sight for the blind,*
> *to set the oppressed free,*
> > *to proclaim the year of the Lord's favor.*

This declaration refers to Isaiah 61:1–2, which also includes *"He has sent me to bind up the brokenhearted."*

Does this job description seem easy and light? It sounds like a pretty heavy burden to me—like a "grand mission statement" to change the whole world and everyone in it by preaching and proclaiming, releasing prisoners, binding up broken hearts, and healing physical infirmities. This mission far surpasses any purpose in life we might take on. Yet

Jesus said His yoke was easy and light. If we are to put on His yoke, what does that mean for our lives and our callings? How did He carry this high and holy calling without being burdened and heavy laden? How can we carry our callings, our yokes, in life the same way? This leads us to the next instruction from Jesus.

"Learn of Me—learn from Me"

The preposition for this invitation is translated as both "of" and "from." They both fit. The point is that Jesus is the One who will teach us how to carry our yokes in the same way He did—with ease and lightness. How do we learn *of* Jesus and *from* Jesus? Not the institutional Jesus or the principles about Jesus, but Jesus the person, the gentle and humble One, the meek and lowly One?

Of Jesus. The only place we can learn *of* Jesus is in the written Gospels—Matthew, Mark, Luke, John—and the beginning of Acts. We can also learn *of* Jesus from those who encountered Him two thousand years ago and who wrote down what they observed in the rest of the New Testament. As I mentioned in Chapter 11, we learn *of* Jesus from the *logos* of the Scriptures, the written words. Here is where we learn *of* Jesus—the healer, the teacher, the friend, the way, the truth, the life, the resurrection. We learn *of* Jesus who invited "sinners" to dine with Him, who saw the outcast, the broken, the lonely, and who touched them with His love and power. We find out what He taught and how He treated people. We see His dependence on God, His Father, and how He did what His Father told Him to do. We learn how He handled struggles, grief, being misunderstood, facing death, and being betrayed by His closest friends—how He faced things we face in our everyday lives that can make us weary. To learn *of* Jesus, we need to expose ourselves to the Gospel accounts of Him—and then we will know more clearly how we can live as He lived and how He carried His yoke.

One of the best methods I've used for learning *of* Jesus is Project 89, so named by Jeff because there are eighty-nine chapters in the four Gospels. Here's how it works: Starting with a new, lined journal with at least ninety-two pages, create a "table of contents" on the first few pages. On the left margin, write down all the chapters of the Gospels in a row: Matthew 1, 2, 3, etc.—leaving the rest of the line by each chapter number blank. Begin with reading Matthew 1 and then go all the way through to John 21, reading only one chapter at a time whenever you do this. Read each chapter prayerfully, slowly, and with your heart as well as your mind. Notice what jumps out at you. A word? A phrase? A question? A struggle? A reaction? A Holy Aha? And what do you learn about Jesus? Write out your reflections, but only on one page of your journal. Then—and this is the key—create a title for the chapter and write it at the top of the page *and* in your table of contents. This title should capture what you observed about Jesus and what you learned for yourself. Make it simple and pithy. When you've read through all eighty-nine chapters and created titles for each one, you now have your own story, your own book, your own "gospel." You will have learned *of* Jesus by reading through the accounts of His life and by reflecting on them personally and prayerfully. As you do so, you will have a clearer sense of what it means to follow in His ways.

My friend and author Emily Lex described her personal experience of Project 89 in her book *Freely and Lightly: God's Gracious Invitation to a Life of Quiet Confidence*: "As I look back through the journal, I clearly see the messages I needed to hear directly from God. I needed to know more than just the Bible stories that were familiar to me. I needed to get to know the One in those stories. I needed to see that he is good, kind, compassionate, and responsive."[6]

From Jesus. Remember that the other meaning of "word" is *rhema*—hearing the Scriptures and the voice of the Spirit in a personal way. We learn *from* Jesus by listening to Him with the Spirit that lives in us. This means we have to pause, slow down, and reflect. It means coming to Jesus to learn and be led. It means asking Jesus questions and listening in our spirits for the answers. *What do You want me to know right now, Lord? How should I handle this situation, Lord? What should I do now, Lord?* Just as Jesus listened to the Father and did what He was told, we can live that way as well. But, it takes time, trust, and intentionality.

Emily Lex additionally shared about pausing and listening for herself as she completed her experience with Project 89: "I needed to be honest about my shortcomings— including my entanglement with the worries of the world. I needed to spend time with him, quietly and intentionally, and prioritize this practice in my life. I needed to remember his promises. I needed to slow down and talk to him and *listen.* Because just as I had hoped, he did have things to say to me. I was no longer just a casual observer."[7]

Learn *of* Jesus and *from* Jesus.

Rest for your soul. What a promise for those who are weary and burdened! As I mentioned earlier, the meaning of "rest" is related to *Sabbath rest* in the Old Testament. What does this really signify for us today? Under the Mosaic Law, the people were commanded to "Remember the Sabbath day by keeping it holy. Six days you shall labor and do all your work, but the seventh day is a sabbath to the Lord your God" (Exodus 20:8–10a). Honoring one day each week to slow down, rest, and nurture your life with God is still an important and life-giving practice that would benefit us all if we took it more seriously.

Yet, as I also learned from Dorothea, Sabbath rest is more than taking a day off or doing nothing. There's an ongoing kind of rest available to us. We read about this in Hebrews 3 and 4 (these two chapters are worth a more thorough study on your own). Here's the gist: "Therefore, since the promise of entering his rest still stands, let us be careful that none of you be found to have fallen short of it" (4:1) and "There remains, then, a Sabbath rest for the people of God; for anyone who enters God's rest also rests from their works, just as God did from his. Let us, therefore, make every effort to enter that rest, so that no one will fall by following their example of disobedience" (4:9–11).

According to these verses, the promise of a Sabbath rest still remains for the people of God, not just for those under the Old Covenant Law. It's there for us to enter into. God provides this rest, and Jesus invites us to come and receive it. But what's our responsibility? Note two actions for us: *be careful* and *make every effort*. It's interesting that we need to *do* something to rest. It seems paradoxical that we need to work to rest; it's not natural for us, and therefore we have to be mindful and intentional to enter into the rest we've been given.

We have a choice. This choice is reflected in Jeremiah 6:16: "This is what the LORD says: 'Stand at the crossroads and look; ask for the ancient paths, ask where the good way is, and walk in it, and you will find rest for your souls. But you said, 'We will not walk in it.'" The rest is given; it's available to us, all the time. But we can choose to not enter into it, to not receive it. We can continue to load ourselves down with heavy burdens and carry them in our own way and with our own strength. We can refuse to come to Jesus and instead rely on our own resources. We can deny we're tired and just keep going along the road of exhaustion, weariness, and strife. Or, we can do what the Psalmist says: "Return to your rest, my soul, for the Lord has been good to you" (Psalm 116:7).

Hebrews 4 ends with this invitation: "Let us then approach God's throne of grace with confidence, so that we may receive mercy and find grace to help us in our time of need" (4:16). Sounds quite similar to Jesus's invitation to those who are weary and heavy laden: "Come to me . . . I will give you rest. . . . You will find rest for your souls" (Matthew 11:28–29).

A final word from Bruner that summarizes beautifully the journey *from* burdened *to* rested: "Faith in Christ makes us *alive*. After a while, as we listen to Jesus and seek to obey his teachings in life, we find that his lessons *are* a better way to live, his gentleness *is* relaxing, and his focus *is* refreshing. We find that deep down in our souls—in our *psyches* (the actual word used here)—we feel refreshed and renewed."[8]

CHAPTER 13

From Glory to Glory

Now the Lord is the Spirit, and where the Spirit of the Lord is, there is freedom. And we all, who with unveiled faces all contemplate the Lord's glory, are being transformed into his image with ever-increasing glory, which comes from the Lord, who is the Spirit.

—2 CORINTHIANS 3:17–18

Every time I recognize the glory of God in me and give it space to manifest itself to me, all that is human can be brought there and nothing will be the same again.

—HENRI NOUWEN, *THE GENESEE DIARY*

Jeff and I had the privilege of spending five weeks at Schloss Mittersill, a Christian retreat center housed in a castle in Austria. We arrived broken and hurting, stunned by an unexpected career transition, and uncertain about our future. We desperately needed soul restoration and were ready and willing to lay ourselves wide open to whatever God might show us about *anything* that was affecting our life with God, each other, and others. We were also eager to explore the majestic surroundings of this beautiful country.

On most days, we sat in a glass-enclosed turret with a spectacular view, thoughtfully and prayerfully going through a workbook called *Living Free: Recovering God's Design for Your Life*.[1] We answered probing questions about our past, our feelings, our inner narratives, and our current realities. We shared with each other as candidly as we could, bringing up stuff we had never talked about before and giving voice to whatever came into our awareness. Many memories rose to the surface, even in our dreams. Areas of bondage in our souls were illuminated as we recalled inner wounds, confessed bitterness and unforgiving attitudes, brought up suppressed guilt and shame, expressed our anger, and named our fears—all of which had taken up residence within us and were spilling over in ways we hadn't realized. We also recounted, with deep gratitude, the many joys and blessings we had known throughout our lives. The whole process was very liberating.

On other days, we explored the beauty of Austria and Northern Italy, going on long treks up hillsides, through valleys, and along mountain trails. We would climb high up into the Alps, traversing from one stunning vista to another, taking in more and more grandeur the higher we went. We reached summits with 360-degree views of the mountains, the alpine lakes, the valleys, and the expansive sky. The word "glorious" comes close to describing the magnificence of what we saw all around us and the immense awe we felt within. On these excursions, we came to appreciate two common Austrian surprises. First of all, whenever we passed other hikers along the way, they would nod and greet us with *"Grüß Gott!"* meaning "God Bless." We enjoyed sharing the same greeting, sensing a solidarity in our shared enjoyment of God's creation. The second delightful discovery was *hüttes* far up in the hills and mountains. The friendly local folks who operated these quaint cottages provided fresh cheeses, cured meats, refreshing drinks, and homemade sweets for trekkers like us. Yum! The *hüttes* scattered along the trails meant we didn't need to carry a full backpack of food for our daylong trips, making the journey much lighter and easier.

Our personal interior work in the glass-enclosed turret and our external expeditions through the rolling hills and majestic mountains coalesced into a remarkable restoration of our souls, our bodies, our relationship, and our hopes for the future. We returned home with overflowing hearts and with greater freedom within our souls in every way. We had moved *from* a state of agony *to* a state of joy— *from* inner restriction *to* expanding spaciousness. The Spirit's loving and gentle work and presence had drawn us nearer to our union with God, and closer to our divine destiny of being transformed into the fullness of God's image—as expressed through our individual lives and in our partnership together.

Two words that best describe what we experienced and witnessed in Austria are "freedom" and "glory." These also echo the apostle Paul's frequent exhortations in his letters to the early churches. He often encouraged Jesus's followers that freedom and glory were grace-given qualities of their new life in Christ. For me, the most poignant passage about these two words is found in his letter to the Christians in Corinth. In just a few sentences, Paul makes two astounding declarations: one about *freedom* and the other about our unfolding destiny of *ever-increasing glory*: *"Now the Lord is the Spirit, and where the Spirit of the Lord is, there is freedom. And, we all, who with unveiled faces all contemplate the Lord's glory, are being transformed into his image with ever-increasing glory, which comes from the Lord, who is the Spirit"* (2 Corinthians 3:17–18).

I'm going to unpack these verses and what they signify for us today, but before I do, let's look briefly at the context in which Paul makes these two proclamations. In the verses leading up to them, Paul contrasts the Old Covenant (the Law) with the New Covenant, the one established by Jesus. This is a favorite topic of Paul's, as we saw in his letter to the Galatians where he reminded the new followers of Jesus that they were free from the burden of the Mosaic Law, the Old Covenant. Here again, Paul makes it clear that the glory of the New Covenant far surpasses that of the old one. The old was on tablets of stone, the new is on human hearts. The old was of the letter, the new is of the Spirit. The old brought death, the new gives life. The old condemned, the new brings righteousness. The glory of the old faded away, the glory of the new lasts. The old needed a veil, and the new has removed this veil.

Turn your attention back to *The Drawing*. These comparisons of the Old and New Covenants could easily be placed on it. The characteristics of "Old Covenant living" would be located on the outer circle, the one representing the Adapted Self structures. In this sphere we experience stony hearts, condemnation, death of our souls, fading glory, and a need to cover up. We hear the "accusing fear voice" and our identities are determined by "what we are." We're reactive, in bondage, wounded, shakable, and burdened.

The characteristics of "New Covenant living" would be near the center, where we enjoy union with the Triune God. Here we have soft hearts, fullness of the Spirit, righteousness, lasting glory, and nothing to cover up. We hear the "affirming love voice" and live more fully in our true identity as "who we are." We are more responsive, free, whole, unshakable, and rested. Where would you rather be?

Following Paul's comparison of the two covenants, he made the two inspiring and perspective-altering declarations we're going to explore now: "Where the Spirit of the Lord is, there is freedom" and "We . . . are being transformed into his likeness with ever-increasing glory."

Freedom. I covered the subject of freedom, at least in part, in Chapter 9, but here we'll focus on *where* Paul tells us freedom can be found: *wherever the Spirit of the Lord is!* So, where is the Spirit of the Lord? The full answer to this question is extensive, but Paul gave us a big clue when he says, "written not with ink but with the Spirit of the Living God, not on tablets of stone but on tablets of human hearts" (2 Corinthians 3:3). In other words, the Spirit of the Lord is within you, within me, on our hearts, on the core of who we truly are. As *Vine's Expository Dictionary* explains: "The heart is used figuratively for the hidden springs of the personal life."[2] The heart, our interior life, our inmost being, the center of who we are and how we operate—this is where the Spirit of the Lord is and where true freedom can be known.

Jacques Philippe offers an insightful and masterful exploration of this *interior freedom* in his book with that title. His introduction expresses the theme he presents throughout his writing:

> *Every Christian needs to discover that even in the most unfavorable outward circumstances we possess within ourselves a space of freedom that nobody can take away, because God is its source and guarantee. Without this discovery we will always be restricted in some way, and will never taste true happiness. But if we have learned to let this inner space of freedom unfold, then, even though many things may well cause us to suffer, nothing will really be able to oppress or crush us.*[3]

Read that again! What Philippe offers is astounding and gives a challenging yet hopeful perspective on our lives: circumstances and people, no matter how difficult or trying they are, cannot dampen or destroy our happiness *if* we allow our inner space of freedom, which God gives and guarantees, to *unfold*.

What impression does the word "unfold" evoke for you? Perhaps an opening, a new discovery, expansion, ongoing revelations, unwrapping something? For me, the magnificent blossoms on flowering cherry trees are perfect pictures of how I envision the process of unfolding. I often walked through the tree-lined Quad on the University of Washington campus when we lived near there. During the winter, the branches were stark and barren with very few signs of life. It was hard to comprehend then that the complete blossoms were fully contained in the nubs of the branches, latently waiting for their coming emergence. As the weather warmed, teeny-tiny buds started to form, and I, along with many others, began to anticipate the full display of pink puffy blooms that would soon unfold right before our eyes. And poof! Suddenly, there they were in all their glory!

How is the unfolding of our inner space of freedom similar to the cherry blossoms on these trees? First of all, everything we need is already within us through the indwelling Spirit. Note that Paul's declaration in 2 Corinthians 3:17–18 begins and ends with the Spirit of the Lord, the source and supply of our true freedom. Secondly, the former blossoms have to die and fall off before the next round of brilliant blooms can emerge. In other words, our unfolding freedom requires identifying and releasing former things that no longer serve us or, worse, fail to lead us to true life, like letting go of the seed coat of our Adapted Self patterns. Thirdly, when we go through seasons of dryness and difficulty, the evidence of inner freedom is clouded and elusive. Yet, if we can hold on to the truth that God's Spirit is still present, active, and generating something new and radiant in us, then we can better anticipate and await the freshness of new growth that's coming. Lastly, a pink cherry blossom is a pink cherry blossom that emerges from a pink-blossomed cherry tree. That's its DNA, its design, its "true self." In the same way, you are you, God's beloved creation, designed to burst forth freely with wondrous divine qualities specifically engrafted in you to display. That's the interior freedom we can enjoy by the Spirit within us.

Glory. I think the most liberating and redeeming news we could ever know and believe is summed up in this declaration: *We are being transformed into ever-increasing glory!* Some translations use the phrase "from glory to glory," which I really like, so I'll use it. Stay with me for another word study. I promise it'll give you meaningful insights into what Paul is saying here and perhaps open up a fresh understanding of our life with God and our destiny. He uses the words "glory" and "glorious" twelve times in verses 7 to 18, so it seems pretty important.

What does this word "glory" really signify? In the Hebrew language of the Old Testament, the most common word for glory is *kabhodh*. According to the *International Standard Bible Encyclopedia,* "The fundamental idea of this root seems to be 'weight,' 'heaviness,' and hence in its primary use conveys the idea of some external, physical manifestation of dignity, preeminence, or majesty." This resource further explains that the use of "glory" in the New Testament "is almost exclusively the translation of the Greek noun *dóxa,* [which,] in the great majority of cases, represents the Hebrew *kabhodh,* so that the underlying thought is Hebrew, even though the words may be Greek." Other Bible dictionaries add *splendor, brightness,* and *honor* to the definition of "glory."[4] In summary, "glory" in these biblical languages encompasses *weight, heaviness, dignity, preeminence, majesty, splendor, brightness,* and *honor.* Pretty amazing!

As you survey this list of descriptors, you may wonder how "weight" and "heaviness" apply to the meaning of glory. One of the clearest references to the weighty nature of God's glory is found in 2 Chronicles 5:14, which reads: "And the priests could not perform their service because of the cloud, for the glory of the Lord filled the temple of God." In other words, the glory of God was so palpable and thick and tangible that it stopped everyone in their tracks. What filled the temple was profound, serious, intense, consequential, and heavy. So, the presence of glory carries with it weight and substance.

One more thing, then I'll tie this all together. Paul gives a clarifier for who the "we" is, for *who* is being transformed in this way. It's those who reflect the Lord's glory with unveiled faces. In 2 Corinthians 3:16, Paul says that "whenever anyone turns to the Lord, the veil is taken away." Okay, so what's with the veil? This refers back to when Moses came down from the mountain with the tablets of stones after being in God's presence for forty days. His face was glowing with such radiance that the people were afraid to come near him. So Moses covered his face with a veil after he finished speaking to the people, but always took it off when he went to talk with the Lord. Over time, the glory on his face faded and he didn't need to wear a veil anymore (Exodus 34:29–33).

In our text here, the veil is something that remains on the "faces" of people's hearts and minds, particularly when the Old Covenant is read. Paul says "their minds were made dull" (2 Corinthians 3:14). It's hard to know the entirety of what this means, but the presence of a veil over your face would cloud what you can see and know. The truth spoken here is that "only in Christ is it taken away" (14b) and "whenever anyone turns to the Lord, the veil is taken away" (16). So, those who are being transformed with ever-increasing glory are those who have turned to the Lord; the veil has been removed and they can see clearly, and they reflect, like Moses, the Lord's glory. Our continuous choice on our spiritual pilgrimage is whether or not we are turned to the Lord, with our attention pointed toward the center of our union with God or away from it, as illustrated by *The Drawing*. This allows the Spirit to remove more of the veil that clouds our minds and hearts. Does that include you?

Back now to Paul's proclamation. Many of us might see how the descriptive words of glory are attributed to God, but have you ever considered how they might also apply to you? According to the passage we're exploring, *we who have unveiled faces are the ones being transformed from glory to glory . . . to more and more substance, to more and more dignity, more and more preeminence, greater majesty, splendor, brightness, and honor.* You! Me!

How can this be? Aren't we supposed to become less and less? We've been told that to follow Jesus, "He must increase, but I must decrease," echoing the words of John the Baptist (John 3:30, NKJV). However, this statement is regularly quoted out of context. John was quite a sensation out in the wilderness, clothed in camel hair, eating wild locusts and honey, baptizing people, and preparing the way for the long-awaited Messiah with a lot of gusto and fervor. All eyes were on John. When some of his followers, in a spirit

of competition and concern, told him that Jesus was at-
tracting more people on the other side of the river, John
quickly spoke up and turned their attention to the One they
had all been waiting for, saying that he himself would now
take a backseat to the Holy One who was in their midst. It
makes perfect sense that John would say he must become
less so all eyes would shift to Jesus, and so that Jesus would
become more.

But are we all meant to become *less and less*? Is this the
destiny for all who turn to the Lord? No! The people Jesus
encountered during His earthly life actually became *more
and more*. He invited them to be free, to be restored and
made whole, to enjoy abundance, to know peace, and yes,
to lose themselves to find themselves. He healed, He comforted, He protected, and He cared. Those who had "ears
to hear and eyes to see" became more and more, not less
and less. Remember the woman at the well, the man beg-
ging on the side of the road, those who were blind and paralyzed, the outcasts, the sick, the brokenhearted, the
wounded, the tax collectors, prostitutes, ordinary people,
and those who were seen as "sinners" by the religious leaders. They became more and more when they were touched,
taught, and transformed by Jesus. They grew in glory and
became more substantial and weightier in their bodies and
souls, and even became witnesses about Jesus in their communities.

Like all whom Jesus encountered, we are destined to
become more and more substantial, more dignified, majestic, preeminent, splendorous, bright, and honorable.
And, we are being transformed *into His likeness* with ever-

increasing glory. Not into our own Adapted Self likeness, not into our own self-created image, not into the "glory" we make for ourselves, but into the likeness of our Creator God, as personified in Jesus, whose glory we reflect. As M. Robert Mulholland Jr. says, "When Paul says we are being changed from glory into glory, he means that we are being changed from what we are in our unlikeness to Christ into his likeness."[5] Transformation into His likeness means that ever-increasing goodness, love, hope, depth, wisdom, faithfulness, joy, power, and peace will reside within us and flow through us. As Jesus proclaims, recorded in John 7:38: "Rivers of living water will brim and spill out of the depths of anyone who believes in me this way, just as the Scripture says" (The Message). Exciting, isn't it? I hope your heart soars when you realize this is your destiny!

Even the harder teachings of Jesus are invitations to become more and more of your very real self, and more and more fruitful. As I highlighted in *Self to Lose, Self to Find*, when He said you must "disown yourself, take up your cross daily, and follow Me," He also taught that if we lose our self, we will find our *very self*. Jesus doesn't always make following Him easy, because we will have to let go of our Adapted Self strategies and structures, but Jesus always makes it worth it.

Unlike the other chapter titles in Section III, which all begin with more negative states of the Adapted Self, this chapter title begins with "Glory" and ends with "Glory." Our starting point is always one of glory, regardless of how we feel about our lives and regardless of what we've been through. God created humans in His image and said we are "very good." That's how we begin and we're destined to end.

When Jeff and I began our climbs into the Alps, we set out from some very beautiful spots. From there, the glory increased the higher we hiked, far surpassing the beauty at our beginning point. As the highest of God's creation, we humans start out as glorious and we gain more glory, more substance, more radiance as we keep moving along our pilgrimage toward the center of our life with God.

How, then, do we have any hope of experiencing this movement *from* glory *to* glory? Here it is: "To them God has chosen to make known . . . the glorious riches of this mystery, which is Christ in you, *the hope of glory*" (Colossians 1:27, italics mine). If the Spirit of Christ is in us, then the fruit of the Spirit and the weighty glory of God will radiate out from our lives with ever-increasing glory and substance. This is our hope!

C. S. Lewis, one of the all-time brilliant creators of spiritually rich metaphors, tells a story in *The Great Divorce* of a busload of characters who were able to visit Heaven and then could choose to stay there, rather than returning to their gray and isolated existence below. The tale is told by a curious narrator, also a traveler on the bus, who recounts various scenes of how the people reacted to what they encountered in Heaven. He noted two kinds of people throughout the story: those he called Ghosts, and others who were Bright, Solid—or Spirit—People.

The Ghosts were the ones traveling on the bus to survey their possible new location. The narrator noticed they were transparent, unsubstantial, vaporous, and rather weightless, so much so that even the blades of heavenly grass pained their feet and the whole heavenly experience was too "loud" for them to take in. The manner in which the various characters and conversations were portrayed by the observer is quite humorous, but painfully sobering and real. As I read through this allegory again, I was amused by representations of the Adapted Self patterns of all the Enneagram types. The Ghosts were judgmental, resentful, prideful, image-conscious, envious, self-pitying, skeptical, suspicious, fearful, lustful, demanding, and lazy. The common stance for most of the Ghosts was their unwillingness to let go of their cherished attachments, attitudes, and adaptations in order to receive the magnificent love, joy, and freedom they were being offered. They just didn't want to give up all they were clinging to, and therefore couldn't see how much these were actually hurting them and preventing them from experiencing the freedom and glory they really wanted. Many of the Ghosts returned to the gray town (a picture of Hell) because they refused to give up their treasured entitlements and their narrow and errant beliefs.

The other group was made up of the Bright, Solid People, already inhabitants of the heavenly realm. They were as their name implies: radiant, substantial, and weighty. They were free from earthly attachments, wondrously happy, and full of love, joy, and peace. Many Solids came to greet the arriving Ghosts, eager to show them all the freedom and delight they could enjoy there. They repeatedly invited the Ghosts to come with them to the higher places, expressing the fullness of life they could experience without all of their favorite entitlements and patterns. The Ghosts usually resisted, clinging to established ways of being and reacting. Whenever the Solids encountered resentment, pride, pity, anger, fear, and such, they would say, "That just doesn't belong here" or "You don't need that anymore."

One of the most captivating scenes was the transformation of a Ghost into a Solid. A vaporous Ghost had a little red lizard on his shoulder that was constantly taunting and tempting it. The Ghost wanted it to be quiet, but it would not. A flaming Spirit, an Angel, came to the Ghost and asked, "Would you like me to make him quiet?" "Of course I would," said the Ghost. "Then I will kill him," said the Angel. The Ghost resisted and also realized that when the flaming Spirit got close, he felt heat burning him. Over and over, the Angel asked, "Can I kill it?" The Ghost finally agreed, so desperate to be rid of this lizard, even though he himself might be hurt or killed in the process. "It would be better to be dead than to live with this creature." The Angel killed the lizard, causing a scream of agony from the Ghost. Then, the Ghost began to turn into a man, "unmistakably solid but growing every moment more solider." The narrator watched the "actual completing of a man—an immense man, naked, not much smaller than the Angel." A bigger surprise came when the lizard was also transformed, into a great stallion that the man jumped on and rode into the mountains. "They vanished, bright themselves, into the rose-brightness of that everlasting morning." *Ever-increasing glory!*

After this experience, the observer questioned the Teacher, the one who accompanied the narrator and explained what was happening for the Ghosts and the Solids:

"But does it mean that everything—everything—that is in us can go on the Mountains?"

"Nothing, not even the best and noblest, can go on as it now is. Nothing, not even what is lowest and most bestial, will not be raised again if it submits to death. It is sown a natural body, it is raised a spiritual body."[6]

We can continue to become more substantial, more brilliant, and more glorious or we can remain in our old patterns, cling to our old ways, and stay satisfied with being less than we were created to be. It depends on our response to the ever-present invitation of the Triune God to *come further in*, to join the divine dance and enjoy a more centered life with God the Creator, God the Christ, and God the Spirit. This is not just a one-time thing, but an ongoing life of transformation from one glory to the next, like going from one incredible mountain vista to another. Since the first step of letting go is the hardest, Lewis reminds us, "It's only the little germ of a desire for God that we need to start the process."[7]

Glory to glory! What a destiny of freedom—to be transformed from one degree of glory to another, to more and more substance and radiance, reflecting more and more of God's image in our own unique way. *Freedom from* the old. *Freedom to* the new—*to* the unfolding space of inner freedom and the revelation of more and more glory along our pilgrimage, one step at a time, turned toward God with unveiled hearts. With light backpacks God meets us all along the way in *hüttes* of love, grace, strength, guidance, and abundant blessings.

Grüß Gott!

Closing Thoughts

Dear Fellow Pilgrims,

Thank you for joining me on this journey! I trust you've received some nuggets of nourishment to savor for your soul from my "pot of soup," a simmering collection of timeless truths, sacred stories, and holy inspirations. It has been my honor to prepare this meal and offer it to you with the hopeful prayer that it will provide sustenance and strength for your ongoing pilgrimage toward inner soul restoration, the reclamation of your Authentic Self, and a more centered life with God.

I opened this book with a bold proposal—to introduce a fresh paradigm: a Centered Set perspective that goes beyond what the Enneagram offers, and illustrates the broader and deeper path of spiritual transformation from Adapted Self existence to Authentic living. Let's look again at this image, *The Drawing,* remembering that the name signifies the sacred drawing of our hearts to God's heart.

As Saint Teresa of Ávila so profoundly expressed, "The process of the spiritual life consists of an inward journey in which a person's consciousness moves from the outer, sensory realm toward God at the inmost center."

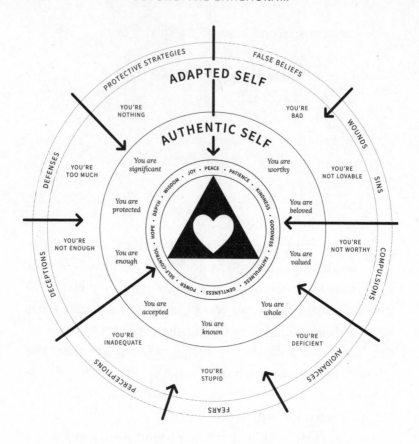

Moving from the middle outward, here's a quick review
of *The Drawing*'s elements:

- The triangle and heart represent the Triune God, who
  never turns away from us and continually draws us to
  participate in the holy union of Divine Love.
- The surrounding circle names divine qualities, the
  fruit of the Spirit, that characterize and radiate out
  from a life centered in God.

- The next space represents the Spirit's declarations to our spirits of "affirming love truths" that describe our true, Authentic Self as created by God. When we believe and adopt these truths, we will more freely and fully express our ever-increasing glory.

- The outermost circle signifies the Adapted Self "bricks" formed of the strategies, wounds, sins, compulsions, fears, and other interior belief structures that create barriers to our journey toward the center with God.

- Inside the outer circle are "fear voice accusations" that falsely condemn and defeat us, keeping us stuck in negative narratives and paralyzing patterns. By recognizing and dismissing these deceptions, we can be released from their damaging influence on our souls.

- Of primary significance, the arrows—not going around the circle but pointed toward the middle—indicate the invitation to *come further in* and that we are being drawn toward the center where we experience union with the Triune God. These arrows also inspire us to continue facing in this direction as pilgrims on a spiritual journey toward inner soul restoration.

- Lastly, as illustrated in the following figure, the Enneagram placed between the inner sanctum and the outer void serves as a portal toward greater self-awareness and greater access to the inner reality of the Spiritual Center and one's connection with God. Although its value is limited, it remains a significant tool for the ongoing pilgrimage to a more centered life with God.

Engaging in honest self-reflection is an essential practice for becoming more *whole-minded*, *whole-hearted*, and *whole-bodied*, so I encourage you to assess where you find yourself on *The Drawing*, and to spend time reflecting on what God has revealed to you in *Beyond the Enneagram*. Ask yourself some provocative questions like the following:

What are you longing for in your spiritual life?

Where do you need inner healing, and are you willing to be restored, no matter what it takes?

Which stage of faith are you currently in right now (see Chapter 3)?

What keeps you from experiencing the fullness of all God invites you to know and experience?

Remember, the spiritual pilgrimage to inner soul restoration and transformation is a one-day-at-a-time, one-step-at-a-time process, guided and empowered by the One who knows you, loves you, and desires to reclaim the one-of-a-kind masterpiece you were created to be. And it requires that you adopt the "posture of a pilgrim," by slowing down, being expectant, paying attention, and being open and receptive to what God offers you.

Before I close, let's look once again at the seven movements that characterize a life turned toward God, a life that accepts the invitation that never expires to "come and dine with the king" and to join the "divine dance." As you review these, which ones catch your attention and evoke a longing to explore further what resonates with the needs of your life right now? I invite you to reread those specific chapters for a refreshed and deeper awareness of these movements.

From What I Am *to* Who I Am
From Reactive *to* Responsive
From Bondage *to* Freedom

From Wounded *to* Whole
From Shakable *to* Unshakable
From Burdened *to* Rested
From Glory *to* Glory

Thank you again for joining me on this journey! I'd love to hear from you, receive your feedback, and hear how God has fed you through this book. Feel free to email me through my website at marilynvancil.com.

In closing, I offer this prayer for you:

Holy and Gracious God,

May Your beloved child experience more freely and fully Your abundant love and holy presence.

Reveal to this precious one their true identity and how to live as "who" they are.

Break through the patterns of reactivity and guide them to a more receptive, responsive life.

Empower them to live in Your freedom, releasing them from any areas of bondage.

Bind up their wounds, heal their broken places, and restore them to wholeness.

Show them Your ways so they become unshakable and steadfast in all of life's circumstances.

Implore them to Come to You when they're tired and heavy-burdened so they can enjoy rest for their souls.

And, almighty and ever-present God, thank you for this beloved child of Yours who is destined to become more and more glorious as You draw them to

Yourself over and over again. Thank You for re-claiming the holy masterpiece of their true, Authentic Self, the one You created to enjoy a centered life with You.

Amen!

GRATITUDES

The one person who stands above all the rest in who to thank for the content and completion of this book is my husband, Jeff. Not only has he patiently walked with me through the arduous process of writing—serving as my sounding board, making suggestions, reading through the manuscript, and picking up a lot of pieces in our daily lives—he has taught me and formed me and inspired me for the last fifty years. Thank you, dear Jeff, for your devotion to God, for seeking your own wholeness, for loving and sharing the Scriptures, for your service to God's people, and especially for being the best companion I could ever ask for on the adventure of our life together.

I am deeply grateful for the many, many people that God has brought into my life throughout my lifetime to nurture my faith, encourage my gifts, and lovingly be my friend. The list is too long to recount here, but I hold each of you dear to my heart and with such gratitude for the gifts of grace you are to me.

I am forever grateful for the blessings of my family! Thank you, Dad, for showing me the value of relationships and how to live into your one hundredth year with joy, patience, a positive attitude, and determination. And thank you, Mom, for always being in my corner and for your loving service in the world. I know you are cheering me on from heaven. You are both my heroes!

Thank you, Charlie and Nancy, for welcoming Dad into your home, for helping him write his autobiography, and for caring for him in such tangible and thoughtful ways. I am forever grateful for the sacrifices you've made to see that his last years will be good years. And your daily care for him freed me up to write this book.

And, most importantly, to our dear children, Kristen, Emily, JJ, and Kurt, and our grandchildren, Nathan, Kendall, Chase, Seth, Kaleb, Josiah, Olivia, Owen, Nora, Anna, and Henry—you each warm and inspire my heart in your own special and powerful ways. Thank you for being strong, gritty, fun, courageous, honest, and channels of pure joy to me. I love you each with all my heart and am so thankful to be your Mom and Mimi.

And, a special thank-you to the following people who have supported me as I wrote this book— you buoyed me with your prayers, encouragement, patience, input, and love.

Thank you, Keren Baltzer. This book would not exist if you hadn't contacted me about writing another book after *Self to Lose, Self to Find*. Thank you for believing I had something to say that the world needed to hear and taking a chance on me. I'm sure there were times you wondered where this book was going, but you kept encouraging and prodding me along. And thank you for your editing expertise and the suggestions that always improved my content.

Thank you to the many talented and dedicated people at Random House and Convergent who touched and created this book in ways I will never know. Your tireless efforts to take my words and ideas and form them into this final product are deeply appreciated.

Thank you, dear Vicki, for our lifelong friendship, for your prayers and love, for the weekly calls that anchor me, and for always pointing me to Jesus. You are a treasure and I look forward to growing older together!

Thank you, praying friends, who received my email updates and offered your prayers on my behalf. I name all of you here because you each carried me through in your own special way, not only for this book but in my life! Writing this has not always been an easy process, and I always felt the undergirding strength and peace of your prayers and encouragement. Thank you Janet, Marilyn, Beth, Pam, Barb, Linda, Sheri, Terri, Lorna, Becky, Patty, Nancy, Francie, Ginnie, Betsey, Micki, Debbie, Jill, Pattei, Betsy, Katy, Mary Beth, Keli, Anne, Sheryl, and Sydney.

Thank you also to the "advisory group" that helped me get started, meeting together to share your wisdom, counsel, and input, along with offering your ongoing prayers: Ahshua, Katelyn, Michael, Mary Charles, John, Dave, Barb, Jeff, and Chris.

Thank you to those who thoughtfully read through my manuscript: Nancy and Randy Rowland, Mary Charles Heath, Beth Barrett, Vicki Barram, and Jeff. Your wise feedback and enthusiasm for the content was just what I needed, and always at just the right time.

Thank you, Julie Jensen, for the pendant, for your

prayers, and for your timely message about a pot of soup. Also, thank you for the books you recommended to me over the years; many of them became my favorites and are quoted here. I trust you're smiling from heaven and continuing to cheer me on. I miss you, dear friend.

Thank you, Martin and Beth, for your holy hospitality, for allowing me to camp out in your cottage for several weeks to ponder and write, for your wisdom, and for your lessons about seawalls and life.

Thank you Gordy and Peggy Anderson, Scott and Pattei Hardman, Art and Janet Kopicky, and Randy and Nancy Rowland for faithfully meeting as a couple's group for over thirty years. Thank you, especially, for patiently listening to me repeatedly talk about this book. Also, thank you, Art and Janet, for sharing your insights about the nature of pilgrimage.

Thank you to all those I've met with for Spiritual Direction over the last five years. It has been a holy honor to be a part of your sacred story. You have inspired me and taught me in countless ways. And I'm especially grateful to those who allowed me to share one of their Holy Aha moments in this book; these breakthroughs are evidence of God's restorative love and healing, and I know will continue to be a source of hope for others.

Thank you to the team at Averson Creative for listening so carefully to me, catching my vision, and holding my hand through the complex world of marketing. Thank you, Brooke Levine, for masterfully creating *The Drawing* images. Thank you, Sena Hughes Lauer, for gently guiding me in the social media world and for your creative ideas. Thank you, Amanda Muchmore Parker, for your photographic artistry. You three women have been so helpful in so many ways!

Thank you, Open Door Sisters, for opening up your hearts to me and sharing your wisdom, inspiration, support, and love. You are amazing women who offer so much in the world, and I have learned so much from your expertise, your passion, and especially your courage to follow God wholeheartedly along the path of your calling.

Thank you, Paula Mitchell, for guiding me and a group of others in the "listening group process" ten years ago. Your wisdom established the monthly Listening Group where I continue to hear the words of scripture and sense the move of the Spirit in my life. Thank you, Ginnie, Micki, Betsey, and Katy, for your faithful presence and openness to listening to God together. I also remember Dottie and Carol who started with us, but are now enjoying even richer fellowship together in heaven.

Finally, thank You, God—my Creator, my Savior, and indwelling Spirit—for drawing me in, from my beginnings until now, to enjoy the divine dance in the center with You. Thank You for blessing me with such dear family and friends. Thank You for guiding my life in ways I don't even realize, and for the sacred opportunity to write this book. May it bring glory to You and be a source of holy nourishment for many of Your beloved people. Amen!

NOTES

Introduction

1. Saint Teresa of Ávila, *The Interior Castle.* Translation by Mirabei Starr (New York: Riverhead Books, 2003), 21.
2. Don Richard Riso and Russ Hudson, *The Wisdom of the Enneagram: The Complete Guide to Psychological and Spiritual Growth for the Nine Personality Types* (New York: Bantam Books, 1999), 20.
3. Evelyn Underhill, *The Spiritual Life* (Atlanta: Ariel Press, 2000), 22.
4. Marilyn Vancil, *Self to Lose, Self to Find: Using the Enneagram to Uncover Your True, God-Gifted Self* (New York: Convergent Books, 2020), 144–45.

Chapter 1: Inner Soul Restoration

1. W. Ian Thomas, *If I Perish, I Perish: Challenge and Encouragement from the Book of Esther* (Fort Washington, Pa.: CLC Publications, 2014), 144.
2. Thomas, 140.
3. Thomas, 147.

4. Tilden Edwards, *Spiritual Director Spiritual Companion: Guide to Tending the Soul* (New York: Paulist Press, 2001), 1.

5. Edwards, 31.

6. *Merriam-Webster,* s.v. "restoration," https://www.merriam-webster.com/dictionary/restoration.

7. This sermon by Pastor Bruce Larson can be found in the archives of University Presbyterian Church at https://upc.sermon.net/main/main/7083009.

8. Edwards, *Spiritual Director,* 78.

9. Catherine Whitmire, *Practicing Peace: A Devotional Walk Through the Quaker Tradition* (Notre Dame, Ind.: Sorin Books, 2007), 128.

10. C. S. Lewis, *The Screwtape Letters,* rev. ed. (New York: Collier Books, 1982), 137.

11. Richard Rohr, *The Enneagram: A Christian Perspective* (New York: Crossroad, 2002), xxiii.

12. Phillip Keller, *A Shepherd Looks at Psalm 23* (Grand Rapids, Mich., Zondervan, 1970), 60.

13. Keller, 67.

14. Keller, 63.

15. Keller, 67.

16. Eugene H. Peterson, *A Long Obedience in the Same Direction: Discipleship in an Instant Society* (Downers Grove, Ill., InterVarsity Press, 2000).

Chapter 2: The Posture of a Pilgrim

1. Hannah Hurnard, *Hinds' Feet on High Places* (Carol Stream, Ill.: Living Books, 1975), 240–43.

2. John Mark Comer, *The Ruthless Elimination of Hurry: How to Stay Emotionally Healthy and Spiritually Alive in the Chaos of the Modern World* (Colorado Springs: WaterBrook, 2019), 19, 25, 47, 62.

3. Kosuke Koyama, *Three Mile an Hour God: Biblical Reflections* (Maryknoll, N.Y.: Orbis Books, 1979), 7.

4. Trevor Hudson, *A Mile in My Shoes: Cultivating Compassion* (Nashville: Upper Room, 2003), 30.

5. Christine Valters Paintner, *The Soul of a Pilgrim: Eight Practices for the Journey Within* (Notre Dame, Ind., Sorin Books, 2015).

6. Information about Identity Exchange, cofounded by Jamie and Donna Winship, can be found at www.identity exchange.com.

7. Evelyn Underhill, *The Spiritual Life* (Atlanta: Ariel Press, 2000), 33–34.

8. Frederick Buechner, *The Remarkable Ordinary* (Grand Rapids, Mich., Zondervan, 2017), 37.

9. More information on Selah Center and the Living From the Heart course can be found online at https://selah center.org.

10. David M. Griebner, *The Carpenter and the Unbuilder: Stories for the Spiritual Quest* (Nashville: Upper Room Books, 1996), 23.

11. Griebner, 25.

Chapter 3: Signposts Along the Way

1. These excerpts are reprinted by permission of Sheffield Publishing Company from: Janet O. Hagberg and Rob-

ert A. Guelich, *The Critical Journey: Stages in the Life of Faith*, 2nd ed. (Salem, Wis.: Sheffield, 2005), all rights reserved.

2. Hagberg and Guelich, 7–8.
3. Hagberg and Guelich, 33, 34.
4. Hagberg and Guelich, 53, 56.
5. Richard Rohr, O.F.M., and Paula D'Arcy, *A Spirituality for the Two Halves of Life* (Cincinnati: St. Anthony Messenger Press, 2004).
6. Rohr and D'Arcy, 73, 74.
7. Rohr and D'Arcy, 11.
8. Rohr and D'Arcy, 93, 94, 97.
9. Rohr and D'Arcy, 93, 114, 119, 120.
10. David G. Benner, *Surrender to Love: Discovering the Heart of Christian Spirituality* (Downers Grove, Ill., InterVarsity Press, 2003), 60, 67.
11. Henri J. M. Nouwen, *Here and Now: Living in the Spirit* (New York: Crossroad, 1994), 45.
12. Hagberg and Guelich, 133, 136, 140.
13. Hagberg and Guelich, 152, 153, 154, 156, 182.

Chapter 4: Stages on the Enneagram Journey

1. M. Robert Mulholland Jr., *The Deeper Journey: The Spirituality of Discovering Your True Self* (Downers Grove, IL: InterVarsity Press, 2006), 76.

Chapter 5: Bounded Set and Centered Set Perspectives

1. Michael Frost and Alan Hirsch, *The Shaping of Things to Come: Innovation and Mission for the 21st-Century Church* (Peabody, Mass.: Hendrickson, 2003).
2. John Mark Comer, *Live No Lies* (Colorado Springs: Waterbrook, 2021), 6, 86.

Chapter 6: *The Drawing* Explained

1. Saint Teresa of Ávila, *The Interior Castle*. Translation by Mirabai Starr (New York: Riverhead Books, 2003), 23.
2. Richard Rohr with Mike Morrell, *The Divine Dance: The Trinity and Your Transformation* (New Kensington, Pa., Whitaker House, 2016), 30–31.
3. Evelyn Underhill, *The Fruits of the Spirit*, comp. Roger L. Roberts (Harrisburg, Pa., Morehouse, 1982), 12.
4. Ibid., 14.
5. Randy L. Rowland, *The Sins We Love: Embracing Brokenness, Hoping for Wholeness* (New York: Doubleday, 2000), 32.
6. Howard Thurman, "The Sound of the Genuine," (commencement address, Spelman College, Atlanta, Ga., 1980).
7. Saint Teresa of Ávila, 45.
8. "Consolation and Desolation," Jesuit Schools Network, https://jesuitschoolsnetwork.org/wp-content/uploads/2020/01/Consolation-and-Desolation_Revised.pdf.
9. Jeff Imbach, *The River Within: Loving God, Living Passionately* (Abbotsford, B.C.: Fresh Wind Press, 2006), 55.

10. "The Gospel in Chairs," a presentation by Brad Jersak, can be found on YouTube at https://www.youtube.com /watch?v=D0BUFR9wSko.

11. Gerald G. May, M.D., *The Dark Night of the Soul: A Psychiatrist Explores the Connection Between Darkness and Spiritual Growth* (New York: HarperCollins, 2004), 53.

Chapter 7: *From* What I Am *to* Who I Am

1. Permission to share this exercise from the online course Becoming What You Believe was granted by Donna Winship. The full presentation can be found at https://www .identityexchange.com/BecomingWhatYouBelieve.

Chapter 8: *From* Reactive *to* Responsive

1. Catherine Thorpe, M.A., *The Healing Timeline: God's Shalom for the Past, Present, and Future* (Bellevue, Wash.: Timeline Press, 2008), 42–44.

Chapter 9: *From* Bondage *to* Freedom

1. Dr. Jerome D. Lubbe, *The Brain-Based Enneagram: you are not A number* (Atlanta, GA: Thrive Neuro Health, 2020), 7.

2. Major W. Ian Thomas, *The Saving Life of Christ* (Grand Rapids, Mich., Zondervan, 1961), 20.

Chapter 10: *From* Wounded *to* Whole

1. *The Connection Between Your Earthly Parents and Your Heavenly Father*, Relationship IQ Blog, Pepperdine Boone Center for the Family. June 16, 2020, https://boonecenter .pepperdine.edu/relationship-iq/blog/posts/connection _between_your_earthly_parents_and_your_heavenly _father.htm.

Chapter 11: *From* Shakable *to* Unshakable

1. Alexandra Kuykendall, *Seeking Out Goodness: Finding the True and Beautiful All Around You* (Grand Rapids, Mich., Baker Books, 2021), 145–46.
2. "The F Word: Forgiveness and Its Imitations," The National Association for Christian Recovery, https://www .nacr.org/resource-center-on-emotional-and-relational -health/the-f-word-forgiveness-and-its-imitations.

Chapter 12: *From* Burdened *to* Rested

1. Frederick Dale Bruner, *Matthew: A Commentary,* vol. 1, *The Christbook, Matthew 1–12* (Grand Rapids, Mich., William B. Eerdmans 2007), 537.
2. Blue Letter Bible, s.v. "*anapauo*," https://www.blueletter bible.org/lexicon/g373/kjv/tr/0-1/.
3. Blue Letter Bible.
4. Bruner, *Matthew,* 538.
5. Bruner, 539.

6. Emily Lex, *Freely and Lightly: God's Gracious Invitation to a Life of Quiet Confidence* (Eugene, Ore.: Harvest House, 2021), 185.

7. Lex, 185.

8. Bruner, *Matthew*, 540.

Chapter 13: *From Glory to Glory*

1. Mike Riches, *Living Free: Recovering God's Design for Your Life*, (Gig Harbor, Wash., Sycamore, 2008).

2. Blue Letter Bible, s.v. "*kardia*," https://www.blueletterbible.org/lexicon/g2588/esv/mgnt/0-1/.

3. Jacques Phillippe, *Interior Freedom* (New York: Scepter, 2002), 9.

4. *International Standard Bible Encyclopedia*, https://www.internationalstandardbible.com/.

5. M. Robert Mulholland Jr., *The Deeper Journey: The Spirituality of Discovering Your True Self* (Downers Grove, Ill., InterVarsity Press, 2006), 15.

6. C. S. Lewis, *The Great Divorce* (New York: MacMillan, 1946), 98–104.

7. Lewis, 91.

About the Author

MARILYN VANCIL is a certified Enneagram Professional in the Narrative Tradition through Enneagram Worldwide, a certified spiritual director, and a trained life coach. She has completed additional coursework on the Enneagram, the Knowing Rediscovered intensive workshop through Identity Exchange, and training on The Healing Timeline. She facilitates Enneagram workshops, speaks at retreats, and is a frequent guest on podcasts about the spiritual life. Marilyn Vancil lives in Spokane, Washington, with her husband, Jeff.

marilynvancil.com

About the Type

This book was set in Sabon, a typeface designed by the well-known German typographer Jan Tschichold (1902–74). Sabon's design is based upon the original letter forms of sixteenth-century French type designer Claude Garamond and was created specifically to be used for three sources: foundry type for hand composition, Linotype, and Monotype. Tschichold named his typeface for the famous Frankfurt typefounder Jacques Sabon (c. 1520–80).

Also by
MARILYN VANCIL

"This book is a gem. It's one of the top books I recommend."
—IAN MORGAN CRON, author of *The Road Back to You*

USING THE **ENNEAGRAM** TO UNCOVER
YOUR TRUE, GOD-GIFTED SELF

SELF TO LOSE SELF TO FIND

MARILYN VANCIL

Foreword by Ruth Haley Barton

Available wherever books are sold